THE GOOD SHEPHERD

A Dart River Novel

Patricia Snelling

Published in 2019 by Patricia Snelling, Inthelight Publishers
Auckland
New Zealand
patricia.snelling.books@gmail.com

This book is copyright. Apart from fair dealing for the purpose of private study, research, criticism or review, as permitted under the Copyright Act, no part may be reproduced by any process without the prior permission of the publisher. This is a work of fiction. Any resemblance to actual persons, living or dead, or actual events is purely coincidental and not to be construed as real.

Scripture quotations are taken from the Holy Bible, New International Version® NIV® Copyright © 1973, 1978, 1984 by International Bible Society. Used by permission of Zondervan. All rights reserved worldwide.

A catalogue record for this book is available from the National Library of New Zealand. ISBN 978-0-473-50162-4

A big thank you to my family and launch team for offering your time and valued feedback, especially Judith Little for her long-suffering, encouragement and editing support.

****

Harold Joyce Cover Art - Martin Joyce Graphic Design

****

Other Books by Author:
When Hope Went South (Dart River Novel #1)
Jessie's High Country Heart (Dart River Novel #2)
Missing On Kawau
Unshakable
Broken Web
Rescue Net

****

Website: patriciasnelling.com

Chapter One

Summer 1982

Mack Reed lolled on the timeworn couch, weary from another day with the shearing gang. He'd been up since five working with his musterers bringing sheep down from the rugged hills into woolshed holding pens ready for the contractors. Mack was always hands on and today he'd spent most of the day demonstrating to agricultural students his own unique shearing techniques. By late afternoon, he was exhausted but pleased with himself. He'd shorn three hundred sheep single-handed. Together the crew had handled two thousand sheep. It was tough and dirty work.

This year, the shearing gang brought their own shedhands and cooks. His grandfather, Walter's long-serving housekeeper, Bessie had always done the cooking aided by her domestic staff, but now things had changed and she didn't mind at all.

Mack took the cushion out from behind his head and puffed it up with his fist. When he placed his head back on it, his mind raced, robbing him of peace thinking about his sister, Meg. She'd got herself into a tangle. Things had become worse at home and it looked like her marriage was on the brink.

As he lay there pondering current events, a deep sense of gratitude about his own life stirred within him. He was now the manager of a high country merino sheep station and married to the sweetest woman he knew.

When Mack had first arrived in the remote farming community of Glenorchy, he had no idea he would be a catalyst for changing lives. He'd initiated the healing of a long-standing feud between his father and his grandfather, Walter who had previously alienated himself from his whole family.

Mack's father, Len had never shown any interest in farming, even though he'd been born and raised on Reed Station. This two-thousand-acre station had been in the family for generations and that trend had almost ended when Mack rejected the idea of farming during his youth. After a long stint travelling overseas and casual employment on an extensive ranch in America, he soon came to relish farming life. He became a skilled shepherd and when he returned to New Zealand he spent several years in the South as a contract sheep shearer. Eventually, he journeyed to Glenorchy where he began to weave his way into his estranged grandfather's life and in time, became the manager of Reed Station, gifted to him by his grandfather.

When Jessie Lee, an adventurous, young vet from Waikato moved to Glenorchy for work, Mack couldn't believe how blessed he was when she walked back into his life. They'd first met at her friend, Hope Rigby's twenty-first birthday and again at her wedding and longed for the opportunity to see her again.

His dreams became a reality when Jessie moved to Glenorchy to set up her vet practice. After they married, Jessie shared the running of Reed Station on remote Routeburn Road, with Mack and his grandfather, as well as operating her part-time vet clinic from a custom-built bus.

Mack now had ownership of a huge station, but his sister had been left out of their grandfather's estate. To make things equal between himself and his city-slicker sister, he'd offered Meg his small farm holding in the Dart Valley—one hundred acres to do with as she wanted. She could now fulfil her dream of operating an exclusive boutique farmstay.

Meg arrived in Glenorchy full of grandiose ideas. She disrupted the community with her outrageous plans, especially the members of the Country Women's Institute thus alienating herself from them.

Mack had deep regrets that he had invited Meg and husband Joe to live in Glenorchy and felt responsible to clean up the chaos.

Chapter Two

Mack startled at the noise of Jessie's mobile vet bus as it rumbled down the driveway. Springing off the couch he rushed to the bathroom to splash water over his face which was covered with dust and sweat. He slapped on his sun-baked jaw his Paco Rabanne aftershave that Jessie had given him last birthday. Pulling his boots on, he raced back outside to give his wife a hand in with her gear.

'Mmm.' She planted a full kiss on his sunburnt lips as she stepped onto the veranda. 'Good to see you're working hard at keeping some romance alive, love,' she teased.

'It's the least I can do to cover up the grubby day I've had today. It's so dry out there and the sheep were kicking up a dust storm. I hope we get some rain tonight to calm things down.'

'Perhaps you should jump straight in the shower.' She walked past him straight into the office to drop off her Carphone with Mack in tow.

He offloaded Jessie's day bag onto the office desk and walked back out onto the veranda. She followed him out.

'Anyway—what sort of a day have you had? You were going to get a new client from Kinloch, you told me this morning.'

'It went well.' Jessie sunk into the well-worn wicker armchair while Mack sat back onto the couch that stank of dog.

She continued, 'They brought me their pregnant Kune pig to check over. They've started breeding Alpacas and want me to come out to Kinloch to look them over. The wool is sold to an exporter in Canterbury ... are you okay, Mack?' Jessie had noticed he'd gone quiet as she bent over and yanked off her boots.

'You're looking awfully sombre. Is there something you're not telling me?'

'Let me take a shower out back if the staff aren't using it. I'll tell you about it later.'

'Good. While you do that, I'll take a hot bath before dinner.' She shot into the kitchen to pour a glass of water, gulping it down.

When Mack stepped into the shower he remembered the bathroom fitters were arriving the next day to install the new shower in the staff quarters. He'd have to drop around to let them know before they fell asleep after a hectic day mustering.

He finished showering, dressed and wandered back outside.

Jessie caught sight of him going to the front door. 'Where are you off to?'

'I won't be a few minutes. I have to let the staff know the bathroom fitters are coming tomorrow.'

'Oh, yes. I'd forgotten about that.' She shut the door behind him.

Mack was exhausted as he trudged along the path to the staff quarters. Their tired yet compact bungalow had recently been renovated on the inside, but he could see paint flaking on the external walls. He sighed—another job to do.

Up till now, the station hands had always used the spare bathroom in the homestead. Mack and Jessie both preferred a shower, except now and then Jessie enjoyed soaking in the old cast iron claw bath. With so many people using the water supply, it often dried up, especially in a drought. They decided it was better for everyone if the staff had their own separate water tank and shower box.

The station staff ate in a dining room at the back of the homestead and their food was cooked by Bessie who called on an assistant cook when required. She'd been a Godsend to Jessie who operated a private, mobile vet practice as well as helping Mack run the station. They couldn't have done it without Bessie who had a live-in position and was treated as one of the family.

Mack knocked at the door of the station hands' bungalow. Coran, a tall, lean man, in his twenties greeted him. He was still dressed in his black woollen singlet and flannel trousers and Mack turned his head away as the shepherd opened the door, thinking he could do with a clothes peg over his nose.

'Sorry mate, you must be dog-tired. I forgot to remind you that the bathroom fitters are coming tomorrow.'

'That's no problem. I wrote it down and I'll make sure I use the bathroom before I turn in. I'll let Ben and the others know in the morning as they're sleeping.'

'Right, you are. I'll see you tomorrow.'

****

Mack had wanted to catch Ben to tell him what a great job did as Head Shepherd. Although Mack had relinquished that role, he himself would always be a high ranking shepherd in spite of that. He and his grandfather had elected Ben to take over that position, now that Walter had semi-retired. The young man had come from another large station, with experience in high country shepherding.

Further along from the staff quarters for the shepherds and musterers was a similar-aged building to the staff bungalow, but much shabbier. This was a lined, corrugated iron bunkhouse for the contract shearing gang. The kitchen had a fully functioning oven and electric hob and in the corner stood a sizeable fridge. Mostly the shearers ate high-calorie meals and used their own cooks.

Mack thought he'd have to talk Walter into updating the contract shearers' accommodation as well. As Station Manager, he should have the most say. *Who knows how long Grandad is going to be around and I'll have to make all the decisions once he's gone.*

****

Jessie dressed and entered the kitchen with a turban-shaped towel on her head. While she stood over a saucepan stirring beef stew, Mack crept up behind her. He leaned over, kissed her neck then gave her waist a squeeze with both hands.

'Let's eat,' she said, serving the re-heated vegetables onto the plates followed by steaming beef.

She poured Bessie's home-brewed ginger beer into the glasses while Mack took the plates and placed them on the quilted placemats. They'd been handmade by Bessie, which she'd gifted to them on their wedding day.

'Where's Grandad—is he eating with us?'

'No, he ate earlier and went to his room. Says he needs an early night and is listening to the radio. He helped us with drenching today.' Mack pulled a piece of paper from his pocket, squinting in the poor light as he read the message.

'Bessie left a note to say it's her day off tomorrow and she'll be staying overnight with her friend in Cromwell. She'll be back late afternoon tomorrow and has left us a smoked fish pie in the fridge in case she's delayed.'

While they ate, Jessie was aware Mack had gone unusually quiet again. She glanced at his face—the deep furrows that had formed recently.

'Come on, out with it! Stop bottling up. Remember we promised each other on our wedding day not to stuff our feelings down or withhold worries from each other. What's bugging you, Mack?'

'It's... ah... it's Meg. Her life's a complete mess and something needs to be done before it falls apart—but I don't know what.' He rubbed his eyes at the same time, trying to relieve the tension.

'Why—what do you mean?'

'I spoke to my mate, Larry from Young Farmers who lives on Priory Road. He says she's been telling his wife and the other women at the Country Women's Institute that she has applied for resource consent to sell off ninety acres of land for property development.'

'What? But my folks live on their property,' cried Jessie. 'What was the point of them shifting down to Glenorchy from the Bay of Plenty so Dad could manage their farm? What is she thinking of throwing my folks off the land? What does Joe say?'

'I don't know. The last time I saw him at the General Store he was looking rather frazzled and now I understand why.'

'But would she actually be able to do that?'

'I suppose she can. Before I handed the land over to her, my previous neighbours had Resource Consent to subdivide—but only into five acres lots—not a subdivision, as Meg puts it. She appears to have brought chaos into our lives, just when everything has been going smoothly and God has been good to us.'

'Look, Mack. Let's both pay Meg a visit and try to talk sense into her. I mean ... if there are three of us, including Joe trying to convince her that she's going off the deep end, maybe she'll listen.'

'We could do. Why don't you phone your folks and ask what she said to them? She shouldn't be mouthing off to other people about her plans when your parents will be the ones most affected by it. It's your father's livelihood at stake.'

'I realise that. I'm sorry, Mack—I know she's your sister, but she is inconsiderate placing them in that predicament.'

****

Jessie went into their office and picked up the phone. Her mother answered.

'Hello, dear. It's been a while since we chatted. I was going to phone you tomorrow on your half day.'

'That's okay, Mum. I need to ask you something as we've had some unsettling news. Have you been to the Country Women's meetings recently?'

'Oh, no, not for a few months. I've had too much to do around here and the last trip back to Bethlehem made me miss a meeting too. Why, what's the problem?'

'It's hard to talk over the phone. It's about something that Meg is getting up to—something that may affect you and Dad.'

'You mean, her highfalutin talk about putting in a swimming pool for the guests. It won't really worry us though.'

'No, Mum, not that. She's been telling the women at the meetings that she has applied to the Council for Resource Consent to subdivide ninety acres of farmland that Dad manages. Her intention is to sell it to a developer for housing.'

There was momentary silence.

'Mum, are you okay? I'm so sorry to have to break this news to you. Wait till Dad finds out. You'll have to tell him and he'll be devastated.'

'When did Meg think she was going to drop this bombshell on us? Or were we going to be the laughing stock of the community when everyone knew except us? Your father will be livid.'

'Look, Mum. Mack has suggested we all go together and talk to them on my afternoon off tomorrow. Why don't you and Dad come with us to find out exactly what's going on? Meg should have approached you first.'

'She's the landowner. We're just tenants who manage the land.'

'You pay for the lease of that house, for goodness sake! Doesn't that count for anything?'

'I'll talk to your father tonight and we'll meet you tomorrow. Arrange a meeting with Meg, and you and Mack stay afterwards and have some dinner with us.'

'Mack and I will pray for you all tonight, Mum. If we hand it over to God, he'll direct our paths.'

When Jessie got off the phone, her heart sank. *If I hadn't come to Glenorchy and married Mack, my parents would not be in this predicament. Although Meg's actions are irrational, I'm partly to blame.*

Chapter Three

Mack and two shepherds had spent another day in a dusty sheep race drenching hundreds of ewes. His grandfather still worked with the animals on a limited basis but mainly did odd jobs around the farm. Since his last stroke, he'd become frail and his muscles had wasted. He enjoyed getting around on his quad bike overseeing the running of the farm, although he had a reliable farm manager in Mack. The old man could still repair the odd fence and feed the stock hay from his old John Deere tractor.

Today Walter spent the morning with Mack who took his dog, Bluey to direct the sheep into the stockyards where the station hands stood ready with their drench guns. When they'd finished for the day, the two men relaxed at the dining table drinking stewed tea.

'Bessie won't be back until late this afternoon. She left a pie in the fridge made from those tins of smoked fish you like. Jessie and I are off to a meeting with Meg and Joe about an important issue they want to discuss—I'll tell you about it when we get back. Bessie should be here before we arrive home and if not, just hoe into the pie without us.'

'I think I'll go and have a nap before that—I'm tuckered out. It's hot for this time of the year and draining.'

'Okay, Grandad—I'll see you later. I've got to get freshened up and meet up with Jessie. She's going straight to Meg's on the way back from Kinloch after her home visits.'

****

Jessie arrived at Meg and Joe's farmstay. As she drove her Land Rover towards the gate, she saw an obtrusive new sign that had been erected on a post that read, *WILLOW PARK*. Mack's Ute was parked to the side as she arrived in the driveway. He'd arrived just before her, and out of her side mirror, she caught a glimpse of him walking towards her vehicle. He banged on her car's roof.

She rolled down her window. 'What are you doing wandering around out here?'

'I wanted to wait for you. I thought we could walk around to your parents' place first and rehearse how we're going to approach the issue with Meg.'

'Sounds okay to me, but what if Meg sees us first and invites us in?'

'I'll make some excuse—don't you worry about that. Come, let's go.'

They walked in single file along the separate pathway at the rear of Meg's home to the chalet at the back where Jessie's folks lived. Pru saw them through the kitchen window. She opened the door waving her hand directing them inside.

'Come in, quick. I need to talk to you before we go over to see them. This is nerve-wracking, to say the least—especially living right next door. It's a difficult predicament and likely to cause division between us.'

Wyatt walked up behind her. 'Come on everyone—let's not stand in the kitchen. Take a pew in the lounge and we'll let you know what we think about this whole crazy situation. I don't suppose it's worth offering anything to drink as I'm sure Meg's going to do that.'

He showed them into the lounge and offered each a seat.

'We knew nothing about Meg's intention to sell off the land to developers. Perhaps it's best you talk to her, Mack and say what a serious impact it will have on this farming community if prime agricultural land is ripped up for housing. There's enough of that going on in Queenstown and we don't need it here.'

Mack sat on the edge of his seat, as though he was about to take off. The fire in his belly was irrepressible.

'You all know how hard I've toiled on this land to make it arable. I worked my fingers to the bone to convert it into top quality land capable of nourishing first-rate livestock. When I handed it over to Meg, I trusted that she would keep her word. She'd agreed to operate the farmstay on ten acres and keep the remaining ninety fenced off as grassland. I feel betrayed by her.' Jessie moved closer to him on the couch and placed her arm across his shoulders.

'She's just a city woman trying to make her way in a place that's alien to her. I don't think she understood the ramifications of the whole proposition you made to her. She is just one-eyed, following a pipe dream,' said Wyatt.

'Yes, I know that, but we'd better get her to stop dreaming before she wakes up to a nightmare one day. She's getting into a minefield turning the whole community against her. Council Resource Consent issues are a time bomb waiting to go off,' said Mack.

'So—will you try and talk her out of it when we go next door?' Wyatt nodded at Mack as he got up. 'Pru and I are the ones most affected here, never mind the community. We left our farm behind in Bethlehem to help them out. If I'd known they would do this, I'd never have considered leasing a dwelling on their property and becoming their farm manager. Now we'll have to move.' Wyatt spat out his words like a car misfiring.

'Let's all just calm down a minute. Perhaps we need to hear Meg first and then try and reason with her. Tell her that if she wishes to stay in the area long-term, she's going to need the support of her community. They could make it bad for her business,' uttered Pru who hadn't sat down the whole time. She walked to the hall mirror to check her hair, straightened her blouse collar, and joined them back in the lounge.

Mack had grown to admire Pru and knew her to be a fair mediator. Perhaps his mother-in-law was talking sense.

'I suppose you're right. She may feel threatened if we go in with all guns blazing and then dig her toes in. It'll be interesting to see what Joe has to say when we bring it up in front of him.'

'Are we ready?' asked Wyatt. 'I need to know where my future lies as an employee here. I'll certainly be confronting her on that one.'

'Ah... ah. Now that's exactly what we don't want to be doing. We ought to be taking a care-fronting approach, not a confrontational one. Please tread carefully.' Pru looped her arm in his to hold him back.

Mack and Jessie led the way followed by her parents. As Mack approached the door of Meg's home, she opened it before he knocked. 'Oh, come on in. I've just put the kettle on. Joe is in his workshop—I'll call him.' Her voice shook as she called out to Joe.

Mack picked up on Meg's discomfort. She showed them into the lounge to take a seat and cleared her throat which Mack knew she did when socially ill at ease. As a young girl, whenever she was in trouble she would twitch her nose.

'Oh, here's Joe.' Meg relaxed when she heard a thud on the front porch. Joe pulled off his heavy boots and smacked them hard on the top step to remove the mud. 'I'm just going to clean up. Give me a minute,' he called back to her.

'All having tea or perhaps a cold drink?' she asked. The teapot in her hand trembled as she placed it on serving trolley.

'Tea please,' they said in unison. Meg went back to the kitchen for a plate of cakes and placed them on the trolley.

'Before you say anything—no, I haven't had time for baking and yes, these ginger gems are from the General Store.'

Mack could never remember his sister baking and it would be a miracle to see it now.

'What brings you all here?' Joe's left eyelid twitched. 'Meg said that you've heard that she's applied for Resource Consent to sell off some land. We don't even know if it's going to be possible—and I tell you now, none of this was my idea!' Joe's face contorted. He pouted, causing his forehead to pucker.

'Humph!' Meg retorted with eyes like steel balls aimed at Mack. She shot around the room poking the plate of cakes under the nose of each guest.

Once she was seated, Mack broke the chilling silence by speaking first.

'Meg, we just want to discuss your reasons for selling the land. Wyatt has been toiling this soil to make it suitable for grazing heifers. The farmers, with whom he is contracted, pay a hefty price to you because of his efforts.'

Meg twitched her nose again and glared at Mack who knew his sister well and was aware she'd be annoyed with him for bringing it out into the open.

She looked at the floor, pulling at loose hair around her ear. 'The farmstay is not really working as I expected. The tourists are mainly from overseas and the feedback has been that it's too far from town and there's nothing for them to do here. I thought it would be well-sought after. And then there have been problems with the neighbours. I've had a busload of tourists stay recently and when I held a garden party for them one night during summer, the locals came knocking on our door complaining about the coloured lights and music.'

Jessie found her voice. 'Why did they complain—was it too loud? And how could the lights do any harm?'

She and Mack had been praying for Meg, that she would settle down and change. They'd been trying to encourage her to come along to their chapel, but she'd resisted.

Meg continued, 'It startled the animals, they said. Some of the women told me to go back to where I came from.'

That was the first time Mack had heard her say this and felt sorry for her. 'Well, that's pretty harsh and uncalled for. Who was this woman?' He had a strong urge to suddenly defend her.

'I can't remember her name. I think she's married to the butcher next to the General Store.'

'Mmm, I think I know who you mean. Look, Meg—you just have to rise above these things. You can get that reaction in any neighbourhood, even in town. You don't need to sell up and clear out because of it.'

Meg bristled. 'Then there are the women at the Country Women's meetings who have formed an outright clique. I don't like them.'

'Did you do as I suggested that time and invite them for afternoon tea? That would certainly break the ice,' asked Pru, with a softness in her voice.

'Ah ... no, I just didn't get around to it.'

'You could tell them about the horses you kept at your stables in Wellington and the shows and contests you've been involved in. I'm sure they would be interested. You could offer to teach their children to ride.'

'But all of that is not going to make my business profitable, is it?'

Joe sighed, jumped up from his seat and grabbed his Stetson from the hat stand. It was one that Mack had given him. 'I'm not going to listen to all this any longer. You tell the family your plans, Meg. You can count me out. Sorry everyone—I need some fresh air and I'm off for a walk.'

Mack heard the door slam behind him. He wanted to run after him, but he stopped short and sat back in his seat, realising that his sister needed help.

Jessie and Pru collected up the cups and placed them on the tea trolley, wheeling it out to the kitchen. They left Mack to continue trying to talk sense into Meg while Wyatt went outside to look for Joe.

Mack stood up and followed Wyatt to the front porch. 'Sorry about all this, but I'll have one last go at trying to change her mind and then we'd better leave it and let her think about what we've all been saying. Don't you want to discuss your position here too?' Mack asked Wyatt, walking onto the veranda.

'Not yet. I want to find out from Joe whether Meg is sincere about placing Pru and me in a bad position. I'll hear it from him first.'

Chapter Four

Meg was way out of her depth and sinking fast. Deep inside Mack a sense of misplaced guilt gnawed at him. Was he mainly to blame for this dilemma by gifting his farm to this city girl who had no farming experience? Did he only make that generous offer to appease his conscience after having his grandfather's two-thousand-acre station handed to him on a platter—the inheritance which should have been shared with Meg? Mack's stomach started to churn as he saw his part in the conflict. There had to be a way through this.

'Look, sis, you need to understand the implications for me if you sell prime agricultural land for housing development. This kind of pasture is precious and the farmers around here associate this farm with me as I originally lived and worked on it. You'll not only alienate yourself from them, but you'll also cause a breakdown in my relationship with the farming community and that will consequently harm Reed Station too.'

Meg dropped her head and stared at her feet. She leaned forward bracing her arms on her thighs and gave a loud sigh. Moments later she sat up straight again.

'I'm not selling all the land. I'm keeping ten acres around the house and thought I might buy some ponies and small animals to entertain the tourists, but there is no point if they don't want to stay here. We do get some guests, but I expected the place would stay fully booked.'

'You don't have the expertise to do a subdivision, Meg. It could go horribly wrong—I've heard all kinds of horror stories from others who have done that.'

'I'm not doing the subdivision. A developer is keen to buy it at a high price. I just need to get Resource Consent before he goes ahead with the sale as it requires consent to subdivide. When I get the money from the land sale, I want to turn the farmstay into a luxury lodge with a swimming pool and tennis court.'

Mack's lungs ejected a quiet sigh as he leaned on his knee with one arm looking sideways at Meg with an expression of disbelief. *What is she going on about now? Surely she doesn't mean this. That's why Joe was so exasperated.*

'I'll hire a shuttle bus driver to collect guests from Queenstown Airport and bring them here. Just imagine if I could get a heliport built out the back and wealthy tourists could fly in from other parts of New Zealand.'

Mack drifted off mentally while Meg continued to elaborate. *Is she being sincere with these wild ideas, or is it just a pipe dream?*

He wasn't familiar with his sister lying or being insincere, although she'd been revoltingly ostentatious at times, but he began to believe she meant what she said. In that case, he needed to devise a plan to stop her, something that could turn her head and fulfil her instead of this far-fetched plan.

Meg shot into the kitchen and sauntered back into the living room with a small glass of Port wine in her hand. Mack's heart missed a beat to see his sister so strung out. She'd always been well-groomed and taken good care of herself. He even doubted whether she'd run a comb through her hair that day—birds could lay eggs in it. He glanced at her nymph-like body, his eyes coming to a halt on her thin, scrawny legs. His mouth fell open at the sight of the pea sticks that were once athletic calves.

'Do you want one?' She lifted her glass in the air.

'You know I don't drink except for the odd Stout—I'm okay at the moment.'

She slumped into the two-seater couch opposite him and at first, didn't meet his gaze.

Mack was speechless, waiting for her to look up at him while she rested her arms on her knees in deep thought. Before long, she sat up and began kneading her temples.

He couldn't contain himself any longer. 'Look here, Meg. All this is not going to do you or anyone else any good. Please hear me out. It's as though something has got hold of you and set you on a collision course like a motorbike on ice.'

'You just sound like Joe. Can't anyone be on my side for once?'

'Oh, dear Meg. This is not a contest unless you make it a battleground. Quite the contrary. We're saying all this because we love you and don't want to see you get into trouble. If you aren't careful, you could gain an empire and lose Joe. This is driving the two of you apart.'

Meg sniffed in defiance. 'Joe just doesn't understand my concept of building an exclusive holiday resort. I don't think he was too happy about coming down here anyway.'

Mack poured himself a glass of Meg's apple cider.

'Give me a few days. Perhaps all of us can come up with an idea that could suit everyone and create a win-win outcome.'

'No, Mack. Stop trying to talk me out of it. It's alright for you. I can see you've had your dream come true becoming the manager of Reed Station—that's every farmer's dream. But that's not me and I have dreams too. I've always wanted to operate an exclusive resort and couldn't afford to do it in Wellington—now is my opportunity.'

'You're going to continue to get much opposition,' Mack snapped, exasperated with her stubbornness.

'They will all change their minds when they see how beautiful it will be. It may even bring some employment into the area for the farmers' wives who need to bring in an extra income. In fact, I was going to say to Wyatt that I could offer him a position as a caretaker for the grounds if he is interested. When I have ponies, they'll need care as well.'

Mack couldn't believe what he was hearing. How self-centred his sister had become. *Why did she think an experienced farmer such as Wyatt would be interested in doing that?*

'I'm going to have to get back. We've got a stock sale at the station tomorrow and I have a heap to do to get the paperwork organised. Just keep in touch. Wait—the family have arrived back.'

Mack walked outside to see Jessie and Pru approach him in deep conversation.

'Where's Joe?' He glanced around and noticed the women returned with his father-in-law, Wyatt and no sign of Joe.

Wyatt shook off his boots. 'He came for a long walk with me and when we returned he said he needed to take a drive up to the lake to think things over alone. He said he'd be back before we leave.'

'I've got to head home now. Are you coming, Jessie? You can stay on longer, but I've got a lot to do before the stock sale tomorrow.'

Jessie looked at Pru. 'Do you mind, Mum? I need to give Mack a hand if that's okay. I'll phone you tonight and find out what Joe's take is on this whole thing.'

Mack took hold of Jessie's arm and led her away so as not to get caught up in another dispute.

Wyatt and Pru left at the same time as Meg came to the door.

'Oh, you're all going. I didn't mean to upset everybody, but I've got to follow my own heart or I'm not being true to myself. Please don't hold it against me,' she said, her voice quavering.

'Never mind,' snarled Wyatt. 'I think you and I need to have a talk tomorrow about where Pru and I fit into your grandiose plans—seeing I'm employed to manage the grazing contract and take care of the land you're selling off,' he said, slamming his

Stetson on his head. 'In fact, if you don't mind, I'd like a quick word with you now, before Pru and I walk back to the house.'

'Oh, I suppose that's okay. I don't know where Joe is but come into the lounge again—I'll put the kettle on.'

Pru followed Wyatt back inside.

'No tea thanks! We want to go home. I have a big day tomorrow digging up the gorse that has sprung up in the paddock on the west side.' Wyatt clutched at his Stetson and scrunched it in his hands as he spoke.

Meg waited until they were seated and chose a seat on the far side of the lounge further away from Wyatt and stared out the window.

Wyatt continued, 'We want to know what your intentions are with Pru and I. We trusted you, Meg when you offered me the role of taking care of your farmland and managing the grazing contracts. You also asked Pru to help you run the farmstay. Now we both feel that you've pulled the rug out from under our feet.'

'You can continue living in the chalet. You are lessees and I wouldn't take that away from you. I enjoy having you share the property with us, but you could always buy us out if that suits you better.'

Pru and Wyatt looked at each other aghast.

'I wouldn't be interested in staying on here with twenty houses going up next to me. Nor would Pru, would you dear?' He nodded at his wife.

'No, I'd hate it, to be honest. We've lived all our married life on a farm and this is why we thought we could compromise and leave our own property to Tom and help you out.'

'Why not wait and see how I go with the Council. If I get Resource Consent, perhaps you might be interested in the options I offer you.'

'We'll see. You'll have to keep me informed after this. I've put much toil and strain into getting that pasture just right for you and Joe so that you can get a viable income which you are now receiving. I need to come to terms with the fact that you already wish to abandon this venture so fast. We'll be going now. Good evening.' Wyatt, without replacing his hat, signalled to Pru to go.

They whipped out the door and stomped off back home. Meg stood on the doorstep scanning far across the paddocks towards the road. No sign of Joe yet—he'd been away a long time.

Chapter Five

Mack followed Jessie home behind her vehicle finding it difficult to focus on his driving. He felt the pressure of a tight band across his forehead and just wanted the stress with Meg to go away. Why did this dark cloud descend over his happy valley and rob him of the future he'd longed for—or was it sent to test him? If so, according to what he knew from his Bible, it will strengthen his faith and give him tenacity.

Without warning, he hit the brakes hard almost lurching into the back of Jessie's vehicle as she swerved at a hawk in the middle of the road pecking at the remains of a dead opossum.

He had followed Jessie's vehicle too close with his mind still on Meg and her problems. He felt shaken by the near-miss and realised how much his sister's unmanageable life affected him. Jessie continued on without realising.

They both arrived back at Reed Station intact. A delicious aroma wafted out the front door as Mack stepped inside.

Bessie, their housekeeper stood in the hallway wiping her hands on her apron. 'Where's Jessie? She didn't say she wasn't going to be in for dinner. I haven't seen her return from work yet.'

'She's here—still outside unloading her vehicle. We've had a stressful afternoon visiting Meg and Joe at Willow Park, but I won't get into it right now.'

Bessie screwed up her forehead, revealing multiple creases. 'I hope it's not too serious. You sure you don't want to talk about it?'

'Nope ... ah ... here's Jessie. Do you need a hand out there, love?'

His wife with hands full walked straight to their office to unload her bags. 'No, I'm fine. I've got what I need out of the Land Rover and I put the rest of my gear in the bus. I'm running a mobile clinic in Kinloch—early start. Mmm ... something smells good, Bessie.'

The matronly woman stood in the doorway beaming. 'It's ready—your favourite chicken dish.' She whipped back into the kitchen and pulled on a pair of padded gloves ready to pick up the stoneware casserole dish.

'Here—let me!' Mack called, seeing the size of the dish. Bessie stood back and removed the gloves, handing them to Mack who carried the dish out onto the dining table. Jessie came out with a bowl of salad.

Bessie traipsed into the hall and called out to Walter, expecting him to be in his room.

'Grandad's out in the workshop. I saw him as I pulled up. I'll fetch him in for dinner,' said Mack as he hurried down the steps to the corrugated iron building that housed all manner of contraptions Walter had invented or modified.

Mack felt indecisive whether he should update his grandfather on his sister's latest farcical schemes. It could break his heart bringing such trouble to this peaceful, hard-working community. Walter stood bent over trying to repair an old plough.

'Grandad ... I ... um ... dinner's ready.'

Mack raised his voice a few tones higher as he stood in the doorway. 'Grandad! Dinners ready.'

The old man looked up, squinting at Mack, as the late afternoon sun caught his eyes.

'Oh, okay, buddy. I'll be there in a jiffy. I'll just wash my hands in this sink. All covered in oil, they are.'

When Mack went back inside, Jessie had lit the fire. She stood in front of it, warming her hands. Mack approached her.

'Jess ... don't say anything to Grandad yet. I don't think he could take it. Let's just wait and see what happens. Maybe the Council will put an end to land development.'

'Let's pray about it tonight. It sounds such a mess.'

'Okay, sure—Bessie doesn't need to know, either,' he whispered as he saw her enter the lounge.

Walter came inside and stood in front of the fireplace, warmed his hands then joined them at the dining table.

'Did you notice the new fire surround I put there earlier? It's one I'd been working on all week. I salvaged it from the recycling tip in Glenorchy. It's pure brass and has a border collie dog on it, though it's looking a bit worse for wear.'

Bessie dished up the casserole for everyone.

'Yes, I noticed when I lit the fire and didn't know it was one you had salvaged. I wondered where it had come from.'

The rest of the meal continued in a jovial tone. Mack and Jessie kept their pact and didn't say a word about the fact that Walter's granddaughter was on a collision course.

****

Early the next morning, the autumn sun rose over the mountains surrounding Reed Station like a giant sunflower, shedding its laser-like rays across the rolling, dew-covered pastures.

Mack, now a seasoned farmer, was always out of bed first at daybreak. Jessie was not a morning person and struggled to get out from under the warm eiderdown. It was one that Walter had given them for their wedding present, an heirloom that had been quilted by Hazel, Mack's grandmother whom he regretted not getting to know.

Mack leaned over to kiss her. 'Come on, Jessie. I thought you had a clinic in Kinloch this morning. I'll go out and check the oil and water before you take off.'

Jessie sat up, trying to clear her throat as she struggled to respond. 'Okay, thanks,' she croaked.

Bessie was up early and had breakfast ready. Mack came back inside, washed his hands and sat at the table.

'Morning—sorry, I'm not waiting for everyone else, as we've got a stock sale this morning and the agent will be here early, he told me. I'm meeting him at the sale yards. The musterers are bringing in the sheep right now. I believe you're giving them breakfast this morning.' He slurped at his coffee in a stoneware mug.

'That's no problem—I'm all organised. I'll have Gina, my kitchen help from next door here all morning. Have some eggs before you rush out the door.'

'You know how to take care of a man, Bessie. My wife doesn't know how well-off she is. Mind you—she could melt any man's heart with her culinary skills,' he said, winking at Bessie. 'I just hope she doesn't forget how to use them.' Bessie flicked a tea-towel at him.

He scoffed his last piece of toast and gulped his coffee. After bolting his meal, he shot out the front door.

Jessie trudged into the lounge in her candlewick dressing gown. 'Morning, Bessie. Mack said he had to fly out the door to meet the stock agent. I hope he ate something.'

'He sure did. He wolfed down a plate of eggs and bacon. I hope he doesn't get indigestion the way he devoured it. Are you ready for yours?' Bessie looked Jessie over as she placed a pot of tea in front of her. Still half-asleep, Jessie picked up her Royal Albert china cup and started pouring the tea. 'Oh, sorry, I don't think I could eat anything at the moment.'

'Are you alright? You're looking a bit peaky, my girl.' The woman's eyes fixated on Jessie, as she reached for the milk.

'I'm not sure—I felt a bit nauseated when I got out of bed. It couldn't have been anything I've eaten as we all ate the same food last night. I don't feel like taking the bus out to Kinloch today, but I have a couple of clients with urgent needs.'

As soon as she said that, she ran to the bathroom and came out a few minutes later bumping into Bessie standing in the hallway waiting for her.

'You've been sick in there, haven't you? At least, that's what it sounded like,' she said, gently grasping her arm and looking her in the eye. 'Do you think you should be back in bed?'

'No, I feel a bit better now. I've felt off for the last few days but today is the worst.' Jessie clasped her hips arching her back.

'I'll just take it slowly and I can cancel the last client if it's too much. I've been feeling tired lately—I mean, more than usual.'

'Well, just get checked out if it continues. Perhaps you could visit that new doctor in Glenorchy.'

'Don't worry—I'll do that if it persists. I'm going to dress and get out the door now, Bessie. I hear you've got a handful of men to feed at lunchtime. I'm sorry I'm not going to be here to help you.'

'I've got Gina coming from next door. You just get on and worry about yourself. I've made you a packed lunch if you feel like eating anything later.'

'We're so fortunate to have you. Where's Grandad—I haven't seen him yet?'

'He went out early to help the men get the sheep in and took his dogs with him.'

'He's amazing, isn't he? I don't know where he gets the energy at his age.'

Jessie rushed off and dressed, gathered up her medical bag, and scurried out the front door passing Bessie who thrust a lunchbox into her other hand.

'Thanks, Bessie. See you later.'

Just as she opened the front door to go out, the phone rang. 'Drat. Just at the wrong time,' Jessie muttered. She waited a few minutes to see if Bessie answered it but it kept on ringing. Bessie must have gone out the back she thought and scurried into the lounge to answer it.

It was Meg on the phone. Joe had returned home and announced he was leaving her.

'That's awful, Meg, I'm so sorry it has come to this—I'll get Mack to call you when he comes in. Perhaps he can change Joe's mind. He had a meeting with a stock agent and left early this morning.'

Jessie put the phone back on the receiver after a short conversation and hurried out the door.

Chapter Six

Autumn

Mack sat in his armchair next to Walter warming his feet in front of the fire. The two men were worn out. The snow had fallen in the hills and the shepherds had gathered the sheep from the steep ridges into the valley earlier. Mack and Walter herded them into the paddocks onto the flat ground, although their dogs did most of the work.

Today was different from most days. The weather forecast spelt possible snowstorms in the high country and the sheep needed to be protected. There was more shelter in the way of trees and large, open barns lower down. The temperature was unusually chilly for autumn. Mack had made sure to check that the dogs had their covers on for the night in their kennels, as well as the horses.

Jessie arrived home late. She parked the bus in the large metal garage and came up the steps carrying her medical bag. She rushed inside like a fleeting tornado.

'Hi, love! Mack jumped to his feet. Anything outside that I can help you in with?'

'I've got a box of mandarins that the couple with the Angora goats in Kinloch gave me. Oh—and my chilly bin I took for the vaccines. Stay here, I'll go back out. You'll catch a chill after sitting in front of the fire.' She kissed him and took off back to the vehicle again. Mack ignored her courteous remark and followed her out to the garage.

Mack took her hand and glanced at her face. Her pallor was clearclear as the last rays of sun found their way through the gap in the garage doors.

'How did you get on today—were you sick again? I've been worried about you.'

'No, don't worry, I wasn't sick, but I felt as though I was on a sinking boat all day. I'm glad I haven't got any more mobile clinics this week. By the way—I forgot to tell you Meg phoned in a distressed state. She said Joe arrived home after we left but it wasn't until late at night. He'd been sitting down by Lake Wakatipu thinking things over and the situation there is not good. He's talking about leaving, so you'd better phone her.'

When they went back inside, Jessie went straight to their bedroom to rest while Mack dropped the mandarins off in the kitchen. He offloaded her chilly bin in the office and placed the icepack in the freezer. *Please, God. Bring healing to her body.*

He went back to check on her.

'Please don't fuss. I'm just done in, that's all. Tuckered out, in fact. I must have picked up a bug and need an early night. I'll rest for a bit then come and join you for dinner later. It's Bessie's evening off but she left us a steak and kidney pie which I don't think I could manage tonight. I'll poach a few eggs instead.'

'Okay then. See you shortly,' said Mack, eyeballing her for a moment. He trundled back into the living room and slipped a macrocarpa log onto the fire, trying not to wake Walter who snored loud enough to startle Buster. The ginger ball of fluff slinked off his lap and curled up on the mat.

Mack went to the kitchen and turned on the oven to heat the pie, and while it was heating he set about poaching eggs for Jessie. When the pie was ready, he looked in on his grandfather to see if he had stirred. Buster had returned to his lap, purring as loud as Walter had been snoring.

'Grandad—I've got some food in the kitchen for you. Steak and kidney pie that Bessie left us. Would you like it on your lap or will you come to the table?'

Walter looked up with a soft smile. Mack sensed that his expression reflected gratitude for having a caring grandson.

'On my lap, if you wouldn't mind. Where's that hard-working woman of yours? I hear she was a bit poorly this morning. Is she alright now?' He eased Buster off his lap and got out of his chair.

'No, not really ... I'm not sure. She's more tired than usual and her stomach is queasy—probably from rushing around in the cold too much. I've cooked a few eggs for her and I'll see if she's coming to join us.'

Mack met Jessie heading along the hallway.

'I've some eggs and toast for you ready. Do you want to eat at the dining table or we can join Grandad in the lounge where it's warm?'

'By the fire would be good. It was cold in our room—I should have thrown a rug over my legs.'

Mack brought the meal placing the tray on her lap.

'I knew there was a good reason for marrying you, darling,' she said chuckling with amusement. 'What do you think, Grandad?'

Walter sat back in his chair again, sitting up waiting to be served by Mack who had gone back out to the kitchen.

'I'm just glad our family has reconciled or I would have missed out on all this VIP treatment,' he said, glancing at Jessie with a warm smile.

Mack waited on his grandfather first, and once he prepared his own meal cutting a large piece of the pie, he joined the others. 'You just can't beat Bessie's fluffy pastry—sauce, anyone?'

He struggled to get the top off the glass bottle but once he did, he smothered the pie until it was red with tomato sauce.

Jessie couldn't eat the eggs and took the unfinished meal out to the kitchen. 'Sorry, love. I just haven't got my usual appetite. This queasiness keeps returning. I think I'll phone the doctor tomorrow and make an appointment,' she said to Mack as she settled back by the fire.

'Oh, really? It's that bad, is it?' Mack stopped eating and frowned, discarding his light-heartedness.

'To be honest, I'm getting a bit concerned myself. I know it's not a virus, nor is it a stomach bug. I just want to get checked out.'

'Bessie's back tomorrow. Perhaps I can go with you as my day is not going to be too hectic. None of the station hands are away so we should be okay.'

'Don't forget me, young fella! I've still got plenty of go left in me yet. Remember that less than a decade ago I was running this place. I've just slowed down a bit since my stroke, that's all.' He narrowed his eyes and the corners of his mouth turned downwards.

'That's right, Grandad. We know that, and it's the very reason I can accompany Jessie tomorrow.' Mack stood up, rubbed his stomach and gathered up the dinner plates. 'That was a hearty feed. Anyone for a cup of tea?'

'You've done enough, lad. Let me get up and make the tea. It's the least I can do. I'm not decrepit yet.'

Mack and Jessie laughed in unison.

'Sooner we get to the bottom of what's ailing you, the better.'

'I'll ring first thing in the morning. I'll have to phone some clients too. I think I'll take the rest of the day off. I'm going to turn in now, sorry—I might just read for a while. Goodnight, Grandad.'

'Night, darling. You get a good sleep. It's amazing what that can do for a person.'

'I'll be coming in an hour. I've got some bookwork to do after that stock sale,' Mack said as she bent over to kiss him.

Jessie took herself off to the bedroom while the two men stayed in the lounge for a chat.

'It's a bit of a worry, Grandad. Hope she hasn't got anything serious. It's unusual for her to be poorly, as she's pretty tough. Working on the station keeps her fit when she's not running her vet clinic. She does plenty of walking up those hills with the dogs just to get exercise when she's not riding Chantilly.'

'Don't you call her Chantilly Cream anymore?'

'Jessie only calls her that when she's showing her. Around here she's just Chantilly.'

'Look, mate. I've been thinking maybe that Jessie could be ... you know ... in the family way. It's possible, isn't it?'

'We hadn't planned it right now, but I suppose it's possible.'

'It's just that I can remember when your grandmother was pregnant with your father—we had no idea, being young and naïve—much younger than you and Jessie, anyway. She was expecting for months before we had any idea. It was a right fiasco when we found out. The doctor was miles away and we were living with your grandmother's parents in a small house.'

'Really? How would you feel if she was expecting a child, Grandad? Could you cope with the patter of little feet in this house? And what about Bessie—she might not be able to cope?'

'I would be over the moon. It has been a lifetime since little ones have crossed my path—and Bessie is besotted with her own grandchildren. They live so far away so she doesn't get to see them much.'

'Perhaps we are jumping to conclusions and making undue assumptions. We'll know more tomorrow.'

Walter went off to his room while Mack sat staring into the fire that was beginning to fade. The glowing embers were hot enough to keep the winter chill at bay. He relished the heat and let it saturate him as it penetrated his muscles, relaxing him. Buster returned to the room after leaving it earlier when the heat from the fire became too hot. The overweight ball of ginger fluff rubbed himself against Mack's legs then dumped his body onto his companion's socked feet like a sack of potatoes.

Mack drew comfort from this four-legged friend's uninvited presence. He became mesmerised by the occasional frenzied flames that shot up from the embers, desperate to save themselves as though they knew that death came, then cold.

Could his grandfather be on the right track? It would be beyond his wildest dreams.

Before he turned in for the evening, he went into the office to phone Meg. There were two phones in the house. One in the lounge and a private extension in the office. He didn't want Walter to pick up the drift of the conversation and worry him. After speaking to Meg for at least thirty minutes, he came off the phone perplexed. This was another thing he had to deal with as well as a sick wife. Meg confessed that Joe threatened to leave her and return to Wellington if the trouble in the valley continued following her selfish plans to destroy prime agricultural land. But Meg was determined to build her exclusive country resort at the expense of wrecking the farmscape. Joe needed to understand that this was her one opportunity to fulfil her dreams.

Mack hung up the phone exasperated. He couldn't believe how self-centred his sister had become ... at least, more than usual.

She was even prepared to lose her marriage for her irrational pursuit of a pipe dream.

He prayed that God be his guide and direct his thoughts, asking for healing for his wife and wisdom for Meg to make the right decision to save their marriage. *God, please make a way where there seems to be no way through for Meg and Joe.*

He decided not to tell Walter about the conversation he had with Meg, but he would tell Jessie when she felt better. His mind was troubled but the prayer calmed him.

Chapter Seven

Jessie sat next to Mack in a waiting room the size of a shoebox. The clinic was still in the old building but the construction of the new clinic was underway at the south end of town.

'It's stuffy in here,' muttered Jessie, her geisha-like face resting on her hand as she dug her elbow into her thigh.

'He shouldn't take long, the nurse told us. Sounds like a baby has just had a jab by the sound of that screaming.' She walked over to read the name on the doctor's door, stretched her back a few times and plonked herself back on the seat.

'The name on the door is Doctor Joshua Douglas. Joshua is a Biblical name, isn't it? Douglas is Scottish.'

'Yep. Grandad said his folks knew Grandma's family in the Mackenzie country. Apparently, he's a widower—his wife died of leukaemia.' Mack flicked his wrist to look at his watch.

'Oh, no. That's so sad, poor man.' Jessie glanced along the corridor as the woman with the baby ducked into the bathroom opposite.

'Jessie Reed. You can come through now.' A nurse in a starched white smock called along the passageway pointing to a door. 'Just go into this room —the doctor is waiting for you.'

Mack sat in the waiting room while Jessie went in and closed the door with the nurse in tow. He glanced at his watch again, scuffing his shoes backwards and forwards. He jumped out of his seat glaring at the door of the doctor's room then sat back down again. The magazine lying on the table with a showy Ute on the cover looked inviting. He picked it up, flipped through the pages a few times then slapped the magazine back on the table and started wringing his hands. When he saw Jessie enter the bathroom a few minutes later, he noticed she came out with a small plastic pot which she handed to the nurse before knocking and entering the doctor's room again.

Mack wondered what was going on. *Perhaps it was much more serious than I thought. It's all taking so long.* He saw the nurse return to the doctor's room soon after Jessie had gone in.

Finally, Jessie opened the door and walked down the corridor towards him, red-faced and agitated.

'Come outside—I'll tell you the news.'

Poker-faced, she walked out towards the Ute. Mack felt a rock hit the pit of his stomach. *Something's wrong.* He opened the passenger door for Jessie then hurried around to the driver's side and got in.

'Congratulations!' Jessie cried out. 'You're going to be a father.'

Tears streamed down her cheeks. Mack wasn't sure whether they were tears of relief or joy, probably both. Moisture began to appear on the stubble of his face.

'What? That's awesome news—it's so hard to believe—are you pleased about it?'

'Pleased? I'm ecstatic! I honestly began to think I had something more sinister going on. I'm already two months pregnant so it's going to be a Christmas baby. In fact, the doctor said there's a chance of me having twins as they are on my side of the family.'

'Awesome—let's get home and tell Grandad. It'll put years on his life.'

Mack kissed her, placing his hand on her abdomen momentarily then started the engine and drove off, his face beaming all the way home.

*****

They arrived back at the homestead as Walter headed down the track towards the house in his truck with Bluey on the back. On seeing Mack's Ute in the driveway, the dog flew off the truck and bounded up to Mack's vehicle. It was as though he knew something, as he wasn't usually this excited when his master arrived home.

'Gidday boy—you seem pretty excited. You're going to have a wee mate to play with now.' Mack jumped out of the vehicle and dashed around to assist Jessie.

'Hold on—pregnancy doesn't make me a cripple—I'm only two months along. Really, Mack—you'll have to back off. I'll be working right up to the end unless I have complications.'

'Shhh—here comes Grandad,' Mack whispered. 'We have to make it a surprise. He's been worried about you but suspected you might be pregnant. Let's tell him—and Bessie will be blown away by the news too.'

'Hi, Grandad. Are you coming in? It's pretty icy out there. The wind is coming off the snow on the pinnacles. Let's get inside.' Jessie looped her arm through Walter's as they walked up the steps.

'Bessie will have the fire going. I want to hear all about your visit to the doctor.' Walter's smile had lost its lustre. The strain showed on his lined brow as he followed the young couple inside the house.

Sure enough, the fire was roaring with the brass guard in front. Bessie trotted along the hallway to greet them. 'Just in time for my minestrone soup. That'll warm you.'

'Hi, Bessie. We'll be there in a short while. Mack and I need to discuss something with Grandad in the lounge first,' said Jessie.

Walter sat in his tatty armchair while Mack took a seat on the couch next to Jessie with his arm around her.

'How bad is it?' Walter asked, wide-eyed. 'Tell me the truth,' he said, as Buster jumped on his lap. Walter sat back as the animal turned in circles until he curled up in a ball.

'The truth is ... you're going to be a great-grandad in seven months' time ... our Christmas present to you.'

Walter took off his glasses and pulled out a large handkerchief. Since his last stroke, he had trouble controlling his emotions he once told Mack. This time the floodgates opened and poured down his cheeks onto Buster's face. The cat shook his head trying to remove the cold droplets that buried themselves inside his furry head.

Walter got up and lifted the cat onto the hearth mat in front of the fire then shuffled over to where Jessie was sitting.

'Congratulations, lass,' he said, kissing her forehead. 'In fact ... both of you, well done!' He patted Mack's shoulder. 'Would you mind if I tell Bessie—she'll be ecstatic?'

'Of course, you can tell her,' Jessie replied.

Walter left the lounge to look for Bessie. In a short time, he returned with her carrying two bottles of sparkling grape juice.

'Here are the glasses,' Bessie gushed, following close behind Walter. 'I believe congratulations are in order.' She placed the glasses on the coffee table then threw herself at them both to give them a mother hug and opened the bottles. Mack poured the beverage into the glasses.

Walter's eyes stayed moist and he didn't stop smiling.

Jessie clasped her midriff. 'I hope this morning sickness goes away soon. I can't take time off work at present with a heap of urgent visits to make. But it's a drag working when I'm like this.'

Mack's lips puckered as he gazed at his wife. 'Why don't you call the Co-op and ask if the on-call vet can fill in until you're feeling better.' He stood behind Jessie massaging her neck and shoulders.

'That's a good idea. I haven't called on him yet. I'll go and ring now.' Jessie stood up rubbing her lower back then wandered into the office. She returned to the lounge directly flashing a broad smile.

'He's available for the rest of the week as things have been quiet for him. Thank the good Lord for that!' She flopped into an armchair, stretching her legs out on Walter's footrest.

'I'm having my first ultrasound scan in two weeks. The doctor said I'll be able to find out what gender the baby is.'

'Are you sure you'd want to find that out?' Bessie asked.

'Absolutely—I think it would be awesome,' Mack blurted.

'Me too. I can't wait,' said Jessie.

'Let's hope you have a strapping big son to help you run the station in your old age.' Walter winked at Mack.

****

After bringing in some firewood, Walter followed Bessie's suggestion and took himself off for a rest.

Jessie stood up. 'I'm going outside now. I need to feed Chantilly her oats and put her winter blanket on as I hear there may be bad weather coming. I'll put her in the barn.' She hesitated. 'What about Zoro—do you want me to put his cover on too?'

Mack stood up and looked out the window, peering at the dark clouds above. 'He's already wearing his blanket. I put it on this morning before we went out. I'll bring him down to the barn, but I'll help you with Chantilly's cover first, seeing that you are unwell. We can put them both in the barn.'

'I'm not unwell! Most women get morning sickness for a few weeks during the first trimester. It's starting to ease the further along I am, so please don't fuss over me. Doctor Douglas said that I can keep riding for the first three months because the tiny baby is protected by my pelvis but to be more careful in the last six months. There's no protection if I fall and the jarring when trotting could cause problems.'

'Don't tell me that. Now I definitely will fuss over you now!'

They strolled over to the large shed to get Zoro's bridle and a halter for Chantilly from the rack. Jessie placed the tack into the quad bike's crate and climbed onto the seat behind Mack. When they arrived at the horses' paddock, Jessie climbed off and approached the gate calling out to Chantilly. Although the horse was a fair distance away, she pricked up her ears and whinnied, followed by Zoro who echoed her. Both of them cantered over to her.

'If you give me a hand to tack up, I'll ride Zoro and lead Chantilly back to the barn. You take the bike back first so they don't startle and I'll see you back there,' said Mack, letting Jessie through the gate first.

'I can ride back with Chantilly and lead Zoro—I don't mind,' said Jessie as she slipped the halter on her horse.

'Let me take them. Chantilly may not be used to leading another horse behind. It's not worth the risk.'

Mack was aware he was more protective of Jessie than she appreciated, but he wanted to avoid accidents at any cost. He could still remember the time Hope Rigby had a riding accident, sustaining a head injury. She'd been hospitalised over a month and had suffered bad concussion for a long time afterwards. *I'm not going to risk my wife and child having a riding accident like that.*

After they'd settled the horses in the barn and given them a feed of oats and lucerne hay, they shut the large sliding door and strolled back to the house. Mack took the opportunity to give his wife a cuddle and walked back to the homestead with his arm around her waist.

'I'd best make the most of this—I won't be able to get my arm around you soon.' He laughed, pulling her closer.

Jessie elbowed him playfully. 'Hey—when are the builders coming to renovate the barn? We could do with those stables already and I thought they would be here before the winter.'

'It's too late now. They rang last week, sorry. With all the concern about you being sick, I forgot to tell you. They've been delayed—some kind of hold-up over materials being shipped to Queenstown. Now they won't be able to start until winter is over as it'll be too muddy. I know it's a jolly nuisance, but we'll just have to keep them both in the barn. They'll be okay together.'

'What about the stockmen's horses? Will they house them in the new stable-barn too?'

'I think it makes sense for all the horses to be kept together. That way, we can all keep an eye on them … I mean, during the cold months.'

'That's a good idea. We'll have to work out how many stalls we'll need for that purpose. I think eight—four on either side will be good. Let's go inside—it's freezing out here.'

Mack picked up a couple of logs for the fire from the stack at the side of the house and carried them in. Jessie went straight to the bathroom to freshen up.

'No sign of Grandad, Bessie,' said Mack, as he met her in the kitchen. 'I need to talk to him.'

'He has just got up and went out the back to feed the chickens. I guess he'll be in soon. Looks like the weather's about to pack up.' Bessie bent down with a brush and pan to sweep up the mess on the fire hearth.

'Oh well, I suppose it is late autumn. We can't complain as we've had a great summer.'

'I don't think your winters will ever be the same again. I hope you'll have a bonny child to brighten them up. I can't wait to find out if it's a boy or girl when you have your scan.'

'Well, whatever God has planned for us will be the right one—boy or girl. No expectations.'

Jessie walked back into the lounge catching the drift of their conversation. She pursed her lips and set her jaw in an act of defiance against generational patriarchal tradition.

'Precisely—that's what happened to Hope when she had Bertie. Her husband, Cole was dying to know if he had a boy to help him on the ranch, I guess. But any girl could fill those boots. I don't know what all the fuss is about having a boy if there is a farm involved. Hey, here's Grandad.'

Mack turned to his grandfather. 'Hi there, Grandad. We've got a few things to talk to you about regarding the new stable-barn. Let's go in and sit by the fire.'

Chapter Eight

Winter

Jessie's Land Rover rumbled down the long driveway that led to Dart River Ranch where her friend, Hope and husband, Cole lived in the cottage next to her parents' ranch house on the road to Paradise. The vehicle barely avoided an oversized puddle. It was the remains of an all-night downpour the night before. Jessie thought it uncommon for this time of the year when there was usually more snow than rain.

Hope and her son, Bertie waved from the veranda. Jessie had been like an aunt to the boy since the day she delivered him during Hope's emergency childbirth.

As she walked up the steps she opened her canvas bag and pulled out the wooden pickup Walter had made for Bertie in his workshop—the one he'd been working on each afternoon. After she'd handed it to the child, Hope invited her inside.

'Oh, wow, Aunty Jessie,' the child blurted with a lisp, struggling to get his mouth around the letter J in her name.

'It's red, like daddy's pickup.'

Jessie glanced in the direction of the shed where Cole's red Chevrolet was parked. 'That pickup is still as shiny as when I first came to stay with you on the ranch. I asked Grandad to replicate it as much as he could.'

'He's done a pretty good job. Does he have a lathe?'

'Yes—he spends hours in that huge workshop of his. I'm glad Bertie likes it.'

'What do you say to Aunty Jessie, Bertie?'

'Thank you—I love it.'

He took off inside and started playing with his new toy in the hallway while the women seated themselves in the lounge.

'Sorry—Cole can't join us today. He's busy with the farrier with a couple of horses that need new shoes.'

'That's okay. How is the breeding program going?'

'Really well. We've some new stallions Dad and Cole trucked down from up North. One is an Appaloosa and the other a Quarter Horse.'

'Oh, really. I'd love to see them. Are they in the stables?'

'Not normally during the day, but because it's been pouring with rain, Cole brought them down and put them in the stables last night. We could go and take a look after a cuppa if you want.'

They sat drinking tea and eating fresh scones that Hope had baked. Bertie couldn't leave his new truck alone and carried it around the house. 'I'm gonna show my daddy when he comes. He'll like it 'cos he has a pickup like this one.'

Jessie smiled and placed her hand on her frontal bulge.

'Has he started kindergarten yet?'

'Kind of. There isn't a proper one in Glenorchy but the school has a room at the back that has been set up for preschoolers and they've employed a teacher. There are volunteer parents to help them and it only runs half a day. Bertie has just started, but it's a bit of a hassle driving him there each day. He only goes three days a week. That's enough for him and one of the mothers drops him home afterwards. Anyway—what's the news you have for me? I'll bet Chantilly is in foal.'

Jessie sat on the edge of her chair. 'Better still—I'm almost three months pregnant.'

Hope got out of her chair and threw herself at Jessie, almost knocking her off the edge of her seat. She wrapped her arms around her. 'At last! I've been waiting for you to have a baby so Bertie will have a playmate.'

'I'm having a scan tomorrow.'

'I hope you're going to ask what gender the baby is.'

'I sure am. Can't wait—but either way, I'll be happy. I just want a healthy child.'

'Bertie will be four by then so he will just have to be like the bossy older brother or sister around your new one. He's already commandeering his pet goat and dad's dog.' They both chuckled.

After spending the rest of the afternoon looking at the new stallions, it was time for Jessie to drive home.

'I've still got that pregnancy sickness I thought would only happen the first thing in the morning, but I get it in the late afternoon too. I think I'll get home and lie down. I was hoping you and I could go for a bit of a ride before I get too big.' Disappointment etched itself in Jessie's face.

'It's a pity you don't live close enough to ride Chantilly to our ranch, or for me to ride to Reed Station.'

'I don't think it's safe for me to ride such long distances on my own. Perhaps it's something we may have to put off for a while. Pity there are no short cuts across other farms.'

'You could ride one of our horses and we could go out to Diamond Lake, just like the old days.'

'I'm so used to riding Chantilly now—I'm not that keen on riding other horses—not even Zoro.'

The two friends said their goodbyes and arranged to meet in the town at the tiny café next to the General Store for coffee and cake before the arrival of the new baby.

****

Jessie arrived back at Reed Station happier after seeing her close friend. Mack was waiting for her back at the homestead.

Bluey almost knocked her over as she struggled up the steps with her medical bag in one hand and a blueberry pie in the other that Hope had given her.

'Hi sweetheart,' Mack said, almost throwing himself at her as she walked through the doorway. He was overly concerned and found it hard to conceal it. 'Here—let me take those for you.'

'Thanks, darling—I'm just fine. I'm going to have a long hot soak in the bath before dinner. Mmm, smells like Bessie has a roast chicken in the oven.'

'You're right—I'll take the pie to her. If you're up to it later, I want to chat about something that has cropped up. But if you're too tired, we can leave it until tomorrow. We have an early start to get to Queenstown Hospital in the morning for the scan.'

'No, I'll be okay. If you need to chat about something, we can do it after dinner.'

Jessie took a bath while Mack sat in the lounge with his grandfather. Walter stretched out in front of the hearth with the fire roaring, wiggling his toes and revelling in the heat. He shamelessly bared his two big toes on both feet that protruded through the holes in his threadbare, grey woollen socks. Buster shifted from the hearth mat and crawled under Walter's legs, but before lying down again, spent several minutes licking the old man's bare toes to the bone.

'Cut it out, Buster! That tickles.'

Mack sat back in his armchair amused by the entertainment.

'You haven't heard anything from Meg lately, have you? I was thinking of popping over there some time. Is Wyatt doing okay with renting that grazing?'

Walter had put Mack on the spot. He knew he couldn't lie so he had to think of an answer that would not place him in a predicament.

'Meg is pretty much all over the place at present, Grandad. She doesn't know what to do with her acreage and wants to develop the land so it can produce more income for her.'

'What do you mean by develop? Doesn't the grazing fetch enough? I thought she would be doing well with that and the money from the Bed and Breakfast lodge.'

'Look—she keeps having grandiose ideas then changes her mind. I really don't know what she's doing—it's best to talk to her.'

By the time Jessie had got out of the bath, Bessie had dinner ready on the table. Mack brought in the heavy dish with the chicken and placed it next to a platter of roast vegetables.

'Come—let's eat,' Mack called out to his grandfather as Jessie entered the dining room. Bessie joined them when they started their meal.

When Mack and Jessie had finished eating, they took their cups of tea to their bedroom. Mack couldn't contain himself any longer—he had a burden to offload. He dropped like a sack of potatoes into the armchair next to the bed. Jessie sat on the bed dangling her feet listening intently.

'While you were with Hope today, Meg rang and sounded distraught. She said they've been granted Resource Consent to go ahead with the property development for around eighteen, five-acre blocks. There is a restriction about building on the steeper hills so that can still be sold off as grazing.'

Jessie reached for her hairbrush. She pulled the tie from her ponytail and began brushing her hair. 'And she's still going ahead, even though most of the town will be against her. So why is she distraught?'

'Joe can't cope with it and warned her if she continues to pursue this path, he'll walk out. Well, today, that's just what he has done after Meg received approval for the housing estate and phoned the developer to arrange to meet and talk business.'

'What? Do you mean he has left her?'

'Yep. He took their flash Rover and left Meg the old Hillman she bought at an auction recently. He's driving back to Wellington.'

Mack sat forward, resting on his forearms, his cheeks drawn inwards. He was far from his usual bubbly self.

'Oh, no, poor Joe. I feel sorry for him. This was a marital disaster waiting to happen. Where will he stay? Their house is still on the market.'

'Thank God it hasn't sold. Meg had far too high a price on it. At least Joe can live in it until this mess is sorted. He told me, the day after we visited, that he'd been made an offer to join the new owner of my father's business as a consultant. He'll probably do that now.'

'We'll have to ask our church to put them on the prayer chain, Mack. This is serious and it will break Grandad's heart.'

'I know. I just can't bring myself to tell him. Oh, Jessie—why has it come to this? Your poor parents—what are they going to do?'

Jessie slid off the bed, walked over and caressed Mack's shoulders.

'I know—it'll be so stressful for them to have to uproot themselves again. I don't think Mum will want to move away now that I'm having a baby.'

'Let me talk to Grandad. Maybe they can move into a cottage on Reed Station. That way, you'll have the support of your mother to help with our new child.'

'That's a wonderful idea, Mack. Shall I ask them if they'd like to do that? I could phone after I have the scan. Mum wants to know the outcome too.'

'Your poor folks. They were just trying to help Meg and Joe out.'

'Let's pray for them all and then I need sleep—I'm done in.'

Jessie took Mack's hand as she sat next to him on the bed while he prayed.

Mack thought he was at fault for not intervening when Meg had offered Wyatt the position of Farm Manager on her land. What a mess this turned out to be. He prayed for protection, wisdom and guidance for each one of them.

Although Meg's situation had the potential of robbing them of joy, they both fell asleep peacefully and woke refreshed to a new day full of promise.

Chapter Nine

Mack drove Jessie's Land Rover to the hospital, as it was far more comfortable for long trips than his Ute. He relished the trip to Queenstown along the Glenorchy-Queenstown Road soaking up the immensity of the Remarkables—the mountain range that stretches from Mount Aspiring National Park to Queenstown.

There was not a breath of wind. The glass-like surface on the lake projected a myriad of pastel hues cast by the mountains across the water.

'Isn't this idyllic,' he said to Jessie. 'We're so blessed to live in such an amazing spot.'

'I agree, but keep your eyes on the road. There's black ice and people speed around these tight corners.'

'You're right, and I have precious cargo aboard.' He narrowed his eyes as he gazed straight ahead.

When they arrived at the hospital, they didn't have to wait long. Jessie had done all the preparation that was required and was ushered in for her scan, soon on arrival. Mack was permitted to accompany her into the x-ray room. The technician rubbed gel over Jessie's abdomen, moving a transducer up and down her skin while she watched a screen. Jessie and Mack could see it too.

'Is everything okay,' Jessie asked, screwing up her face, as she craned her neck sideways to see the screen.

'I'm just locating baby now. Hear that?'

In an instant, there was a strong heartbeat.

'Hmm ... just a minute,' the woman muttered.

'What's wrong?' Mack asked, sucking air into his lungs at the same time. He grabbed hold of Jessie's hand.

'I think there is another one.' The woman leaned forward, straining to get a better view.

'What do you mean?' Jessie's voice quavered.

'There's another baby in there. You're going to have twins.'

Mack's mouth dropped wide open, baring a mouthful of white teeth.

'What! That's fantastic, isn't it darling,' Jessie spouted, staring at Mack who sat there in the same position, with eyes like a goldfish.

The technician rolled the wand across Jessie once more and stopped. 'Would you like to know the sex of your babies?'

'Absolutely!' They cried in unison.

The woman pressed a few buttons on the screen as they watched intensely. 'You have two decent sized boys in there—see?'

She demonstrated with her hand the various anatomy of each baby.

'All finished now.' She wiped the gel from Jessie's skin and took her arm as she climbed off the table.

'Could you sit here a minute while I check the scans and I'll be back.'

The woman assisted her into a chair and walked off down a corridor.

'Wait until we tell Grandad ... and Bessie. Mum and Dad will be thrilled and so will your parents.' Mack wiped his eyes roughly with his sleeve and sat staring at Jessie's bump in her abdomen. 'Just imagine two babies growing in there.'

'I can't wait to tell my parents. That'll give them a boost with all this negative stuff going on with Meg and Joe. They definitely will have to come and live on Reed Station now.'

The technician returned. 'You can get dressed now. Just throw the gown in the basket in the changing room. You can go after that and your doctor will get the report in a few days.'

They walked to their vehicle with Mack holding Jessie's hand, leading her down a cracked, concrete path to the carpark.

'It's icy today. I can't take the risk of letting you slip.'

'I'm not an invalid, Mack but I get your point. The footpath must have iced over last night. Let's hurry and get in the car—it's freezing out here.'

Mack pulled out of the carpark then hesitated.

'I thought we could stop for a coffee at that great café on the other side of town near Closeburn.' He leaned forward to turn up the heating in the car.

'I've got another idea. Why don't you go to talk some sense into Meg and tell her what we've come up with as a solution to her problem, and I'll visit Mum and Dad to see if they'd like to move to Reed Station.'

'That's a great idea. Your news about the twins should cheer them up after all their disappointment with Meg and especially the idea of living nearby to help with their grandchildren,' said Mack.

'Maybe this is divine intervention so we can all work in together as an extended family,' said Jessie, relaxing back into the seat.

****

Jessie ambled along the path to her parents' chalet, while Mack disappeared inside Meg's house. She'd seen him arrive and held the door open for him.

'Coming to rescue your wayward sister, are you?' She gave him a wry smile. 'It's all a bit of a mess, isn't it?'

Mack guessed she'd been crying, by the dark rings around her eyes and puffy eyelids. *Rare for Meg to break down. She is usually pretty stoic.* 'Well, I can't just leave you in the lurch. Jessie and I have come up with a few suggestions that might ease your burden.'

Meg hadn't offered Mack a seat so he barged in and slumped into one of her sleek, leather armchairs. She followed suit and sat in the chair opposite.

She pointed at the cabinet where Joe kept bottles of wine and whisky—remnants of their high society lifestyle in Wellington.

'Pity you don't drink as I'd ask you to have a glass of wine with me.'

'No, thanks. I'd love a coffee though.'

'I've got some percolating—I'll bring it in.'

While she was in the kitchen, Mack glanced at a pile of papers sitting on the coffee table—sale and purchase papers all drawn up ready to sign. He bent over the documents to look for her signature, but the dotted line was bare.

Meg returned with a tray of coffee mugs and chocolate cake.

'Here—have some cake. I don't know if you'll like it. I bought it from the General Store yesterday and it's nothing like your Bessie's baking—or Jessie's for that matter.'

'Sorry, but I couldn't help seeing the sale and purchase papers for your property,' Mack muttered, as Meg reached down and grabbed them.

'Oh, yes. I wanted to tell you about it—the council will only allow the land to be subdivided into five-acre allotments and this property with the house can be divided into ten acres. That's what I want to do.'

Mack sat bewildered about her behaviour. *Her husband has just left her and she's babbling on about property development.*

'Meg! I'm here to find out what's happening with you and Joe, not your land. What's going on?'

'He had an offer a while ago to work as a consultant for the new owner of dad's old company. He couldn't accept it because of our move here. He is upset by all the opposition from the community over my interest in property development. I mean ... he didn't have to stalk off like that. I couldn't bear to turn my back on all this.' She stared at the ground then pulled out a handkerchief to wipe her nose. Mack glared at her as she folded her arms on her lap with a belligerent expression on her face.

He remembered how she had always respected him when they were young and how close they'd been.

'But you haven't considered Joe in any of your plans—or Jessie's folks either. This has been all about you, and to be honest, I think you've become incredibly self-centred. I'm disappointed in you.'

Meg pulled her head up and burst out crying. Mack was about to continue when loud sobs interrupted him as she pushed her face into her hands. She blew her nose, making a sound like a foghorn. Mack waited until she'd calmed down then walked over and put an arm around her.

'Look sis—I don't know why or how you've got yourself into this predicament, but Jessie and I want to help you sort it out and restore your marriage. You do love Joe, don't you?'

'Yes, of course, I do. I just can't understand why he won't accept my point of view.'

'Perhaps he's asking himself the same question. Have you ever put yourself in his shoes? He gave up a successful career and stately home in Wellington—not to mention all his friends—to come to a remote and rugged area to live off the land which is totally alien to him. I feel sorry for the guy.'

Meg tried to pull herself together.

'You gave me a hundred acres and I wanted to put it to good use. You know I always dreamed of owning a resort, just as you always had your heart set on managing a high country station.'

'Yes, Meg, but not at the cost of hurting others. You've got it all wrong. Listen to me.'

All through this, Mack dearly wanted to tell Meg she was going to be an aunt twice over, but he had to pick his moment. It would have to wait—or not. He had an idea.

'Meg—Jessie is pregnant. We've just come back from the hospital where she had her first scan. She's two months along already and going to have twins,' he blurted then waited for her reaction.

Meg stopped her snivelling and sat bolt upright, pushing her hair out of her face. Her eyes had doubled in size as she suddenly perked up.

'What? Congratulations! Why didn't you let me know she was pregnant? I wouldn't have worried you with all of this.'

'We didn't want to break the news when Joe had just walked out. That would have added to your pain.'

'I feel so foolish now—I'm sorry. As you can see, I haven't signed the papers for the sale. I don't know what to do. What ideas did you say you had?'

'Now that we are going to need support with two babies, Jessie is going to ask her folks if they'd like to move to Reed Station. That way, her mother can help with the twins if she chooses. Her father may be interested in assisting me to run the station. Grandad is pulling back a great deal these days.'

'Oh, that's a pity—they don't have to move out. They might change their mind now that there won't be a housing development taking place. Where will they live—in the house with all of you?'

'We have the small cottage that Aron, my predecessor had tenanted with his wife—it's still vacant. Grandad was going to rent it out to our new Head Shepherd but he has decided to move into a house down the road.'

Meg looked down at the ground. Her face took on another strained appearance.

'I'll go and talk to them tomorrow and see what they'd like to do. I need to make amends to them somehow.'

'I have an idea—if you want to use the land to make an income. I heard someone at the High Country Farmer's meeting say that Dan Hislop, your neighbour needed more land. At first, I thought Wyatt could approach him to see if he wanted to rent grazing from you, but now we can ask him to make an offer on the remaining ninety acres. If you hold on to ten acres for your own animals you can keep horses. Ten acres is enough for ponies.'

'Oh, good heavens. It does seem a better idea than having twenty houses going up around me. That would make everything straight forward and I'll have the money to put into the resort too.'

'Land of this quality is valuable around here and fetching high prices. Let me go and talk to Dan to see if he's willing to make an offer if you're keen to go ahead.'

Meg got out of her chair and lunged at her brother, enveloping him with her arms.

'Thank you so much, Mack. I thought I could work it out on my own, but it has got out of hand.'

'Well, that's what families are for. Jessie and I may have some other ideas to help you but first things first. Let's get this land sold, and I want you to promise to keep the communication open to Joe. We want to see this marriage restored.'

Meg stared at her wedding ring and pulled at it. 'I'll do my best.'

'I'm going next door to take Jessie home. Do you mind if I share with her parents the conversation we've just had?'

'No, not at all. I'll go and see them in the morning. Please tell Jessie I'm sorry about all the grief I've caused. I'll be in touch with her.'

Chapter Ten

Walter had already finished eating and kept the rest of the evening meal in the oven for Jessie and Mack. Mack walked into the lounge with his meal on a tray and perched next to Jessie who sat back eating with her feet elevated on a stool.

'Hi, Grandad. Thanks for keeping our food warm.'

'I can't go off to bed not knowing the outcome of your scan. I'm waiting for your report—is everything alright?' He craned forward to listen, almost crushing the cat on his lap.

'Don't you have any ideas about leaving this world just yet. We're going to need your help around here with this extended family on its way.' Mack winked at Jessie who beckoned him to continue.

'Don't keep me hanging. Well, what is it—a boy or a girl?'

'Peter and Paul, Grandad,' said Jessie beaming.

'What ... what do you mean—are you having twins?'

'Yep, that's right. I'm just joking about the names, but I have two boys in here.' Jessie patted her belly.

'I'll need you to train them to be good shepherds, Grandad.' Mack threw him an infectious smile.

The old man rubbed his eyes. 'This is more than an old man could ask for at my age. You two are so blessed.'

'They will be a blessing to you also, Grandad,' said Jessie.

'Just wait till Bessie hears this news. She arrived home earlier and went straight to bed—all the driving tired her out when she visited her family today.'

Mack and Jessie spent the rest of the evening discussing with Walter their plans to bring Jessie's parents onto the station.

Walter yawned loudly, rubbing his eyes. 'I think that will work out well. The cottage is all kitted out so they should be at home there. Aron had even landscaped the small area out front, so it should be easy for them to maintain.'

Jessie smiled. 'Thanks, Grandad. I can't wait to show them their new home.'

Walter gave Jessie a loving glance. 'We are family after all and need to look after each other.'

She got out of her chair, walked over to Walter and wrapped her arms around him. He caught his reading glasses just in time.

'No need for all that sentiment, girl. Any decent person would help in this situation.'

Mack joined in, 'Thanks, Grandad—stop trying to be so modest—you're a proper champ.'

'You just don't realise I have ulterior motives. My friends in the Bay of Plenty said that Wyatt has great shepherding skills and sound farming experience. He has been a long-standing member of the Federated Farmers meetings there and is well-known. I think he's going to fill the gap for me when I can't oversee the running of Reed Station any longer—even if it's only in an advisory capacity.'

Jessie patted Walter on the shoulder and sat back in her chair. 'Mum seems to have got on well with Bessie—perhaps she can be of help to her as well.'

Walter nodded at Mack. 'I think we're all going to be a great team in spite of Meg's foolishness and short-sightedness. She has been on a collision course for disaster and you just curbed it. It's best for Jessie's parents to stay well clear for now.'

Jessie got up to rush off to the office. 'I'll call and ask if they'd like to check out the cottage tomorrow. I can't wait to have them come and live with us.'

****

Jessie sat in her vehicle the next morning looking at her work schedule. She had two visits to make near Dart River Ranch where Hope lived. It had seemed ages since she'd visited her friend whom she had phoned the night before to warn of her arrival. Life had just been too hectic but she had so much news to share.

Mack and Walter had already left the house to meet up with the stockmen to bring the young heifers down for Tuberculosis testing. The agricultural technicians would soon arrive from Queenstown and Jessie didn't need to be there.

Her farm visits were over by midday and she was eager to visit Hope who had lunch ready for her when she arrived.

She sat at the dining table with Bertie sitting next to her. He attended kindergarten daily, but today Hope kept him home for Jessie's visit.

His mother handed him a slice of brown bread coated with a thick layer of peanut butter.

'Come on, Bertie. Show Aunty Jessie how well you can eat all your lunch.'

'I want milk,' he uttered, pouting

Hope frowned at him. 'Please! Ask nicely, Bertie.'

He looked at Jessie with a wry smile, licking peanut butter from his fingers.

'Milk please, Mummy.' He shot another glance at Jessie. 'Bertie's going to have a sister ... aren't I, Mummy?'

'Shush—eat your food!' Hope's face turned the colour of her pink blouse. 'He's excited as he overheard me telling my mother that he's getting a sister, but he wasn't supposed to tell anyone yet. Yes—I'm expecting number two.'

Jessie's eyes lowered to Hope's abdomen while she patted her own. 'That's awesome news!'

'How did your scan go? Do you know what you're having yet—boy or girl?' Hope stared at Jessie waiting for a reaction.

'That's what I came here to tell you—I'm going to have twins.' Hopes mouth dropped open. 'What—really? How far are you?'

'Almost five months. I thought my baby would be a playmate for Bertie but he will have one of his own. My twins are both boys so Bertie will have mates.' Jessie started pushing on her bulge. 'Here feel this—one of them is kicking.'

The girls sat entertaining themselves trying to identify the different body parts of her unborn twins.

Bertie came off his seat and leaned over Jessie, staring at her abdomen. 'Aunty Jessie—can Bertie feel your tummy too? Please—let me touch the babies.'

'Of course, Bertie—let me show you.' She took his hand and guided it to the spot where the strongest kicks could be felt.

'Well, now—how far along are you, Hope? You've been keeping your news quiet.'

'Sorry, Jessie. Like you, we've been so busy and haven't had much social life. We wanted to wait until I had the first scan before announcing it. I'm expecting a baby girl in November.'

'That is so amazing—my twins are due in December! We could have them at the same time. I hope you don't have my midwife, especially if we are in labour at the same time.'

They both chuckled.

'Let's go out onto the veranda.' Hope carried toys out for Bertie with Jessie in tow. The boy sat down happily while the women continued to talk.

'I was thinking our local mobile vet could deliver my baby. What do you think—it was you who brought Bertie safely into the world without a problem?'

Jessie could see by the look on Hope's face that she was serious. 'You're joking of course. That was an emergency and I don't think I'd like to be in that position again. You just stick to your midwife.'

Hope's smile turned upside down. 'If you insist ... who is your midwife?'

'I'm under that new Dr Joshua Douglas. He does obstetrics as well as being a General Practitioner.'

'Oh, I see. Mmm. I heard that he's pretty dishy—a bit of *eye candy*,' Hope teased, becoming animated again.

Jessie was quick to defend herself. 'He knew Walter's family back in Lake Tekapo apparently and I heard he's a good doctor so thought I'd check him out.'

Hope continued, 'My other news is our stud is flourishing and I'm now involved with Cole in the breeding program full time instead of running riding courses—I've no time for that. It's a pity as there's no other riding school or holiday program around here.'

Bertie began to entertain them with dance moves to a musical duck while Jessie told Hope all about the drama that Meg had created. When she had finished her synopsis of the situation, she burst forth.

'You've just given me an idea to help Meg! She's an experienced rider from Wellington—I've seen her trophies. For a while, she was a riding instructor so maybe she could start a riding school at Willow Park. What do you think?'

'The only time I've met her was at your wedding and it's hard to imagine her as an equestrian. Perhaps Dad and I could help her get started—you know Dad is a horse whisperer.'

'Yes, I know and so are you—he taught you well. It would be great if Meg goes along with this, but you won't be able to do much with another baby on the way. Mack can train horses and he was taught by your father too.'

'Remember I have Mum living next door to help me. I didn't give up anything after I had Bertie—I've had to reduce my hours, that's all. I only recently stopped running the riding courses and holiday program to help Cole with our business.'

Jessie sat ruminating on the subject of Meg, twirling a lock of her hair around her index finger.

'I suppose Meg could run a holiday camp. She has a huge lodge that is often empty at low season. There are eight double bedrooms that could fit bunks. She could turn that massive barn of hers into bunkrooms for the kids and keep one for stables.'

Hope reached for Bertie's hand as he was about to take off down the steps. She planted him back down on the veranda.

'What a superb idea. I remember when I took my horse to various camps in the Bay of Plenty there was one that was unique. An oversized barn had been converted into bunkrooms surrounding an inside arena. It was so special going to sleep with the nostalgic smell of hay and horses emanating through the wooden bedroom doors.'

Hope stood up again. 'I don't mind meeting up with Meg to help her get started. Let's move down onto the steps so I can watch Bertie if he wants to play on the lawn.'

Jessie couldn't wait to get back to Reed Station to discuss her ideas with Mack. Or should she call by Willow Park and discuss it with Meg now? She had already answered her own question. It was time to smooth things over.

'Sorry, Hope, but I'll have to get off now as I've got a heap of things to do. Thanks for lunch—it's my turn next time.'

She hugged Bertie and Hope and hurtled along the long driveway in her vehicle onto the main road. Her heart raced at the thought of seeing Meg turn her life around. *Was this an answer to prayer?*

Chapter Eleven

Jessie loved the scenic drive along Glenorchy-Paradise Road passing the majestic Richardson Mountains on one side and the Humboldt Mountains on the other. The late afternoon sun disappeared quickly behind the mountains. *Before long it will be dark. Perhaps I should have come another day.*

When she pulled into the space near the front door, Meg's face appeared at the kitchen window then pulled back. Jessie couldn't help noticing ivy-like weeds smothering the footpath to the house. The outside of the home appeared tired and neglected. *Is this the beginning of the decline as it looks like she hasn't been managing here on her own since Joe left?*

The windows needed a good clean and Jessie thought how unappealing the entrance to the *so-called* boutique farmstay would be for the tourist who would expect an exclusive country lodge or something more welcoming.

'Jessie! Come on in. I wasn't expecting you, but it's good to see you.' Meg pulled at the loose wisps of hair that dangled down her forehead, trying to sweep them back up again.

She wore no makeup—unlike her Wellington days when she would decorate herself like Cleopatra. Now it was obvious to Jessie her life had become unmanageable.

Jessie's eyes quickly scanned the lounge spying the cobwebs hanging from the bookshelves and dust that coated the furniture. It was a far cry from her home in Wellington that was so pristine one could eat off the floors. She grimaced—*why did she allow herself to plummet so low?*

'Sorry that it's a bit late in the afternoon ... I was just passing.'

'I'm glad of the company ... coffee? I've just percolated a fresh lot or you can have tea if you'd rather.'

'What about that fruit tea you gave me last time I visited?'

'I've still got some of that—it was raspberry. Back in a minute.'

Meg brought back a tray with a stoneware mug of coffee for herself and a china cup with tea for Jessie.

'I hope you don't mind, Meg, but I've been thinking of ways to help you rise above the um … difficult situation … you've found yourself in.' Jessie really wanted to say it was a situation she had brought on herself but stopped short.

'That's kind of you. Can I pass you a gingernut biscuit?'

'Yes, thanks. If you don't mind, I like to dunk these in my tea.' Jessie was aware Meg would see that as common, but she couldn't help herself. She continued. 'My friend, Hope whom you met at my wedding is an accomplished rider like you and, until recently, has been running a small riding school for children who slept in a fully insulated barn on hay bales. A few kids with asthma stayed inside her folks' ranch house.'

Meg screwed up her face. 'Sorry … what are you getting at?'

'Now that Hope is expecting another baby and engrossed with their Stud, she has stopped running the horse camps and riding lessons. The closest is the other side of Queenstown near Cromwell. Perhaps Hope and her father, Joel can help you set one up here. Apart from them both being horse whisperers, they can give you good advice and Mack or Wyatt might help too.' Jessie kept her eyes fixed on Meg's face.

'I suppose that could work. It would supplement my income after selling the land, as long as I could get regular clients.'

'It was popular amongst the school and university students, and the tourist industry is starting to take off in the area. You can provide horse treks just as she did—and lessons. Riders visited their camp from all over the South Island. I'm sure it will do well as Glenorchy is becoming popular.'

Meg sat silent for a few minutes. 'Come and look at the ten acres I'll have at my disposal.'

'I'd love to look around as it appears as though it hasn't changed since Mack lived here. Can I take a look at the barn over there?'

'Okay, let's go.' Meg went to get her boots which were on the doorstep where Jessie had left hers. She burst forth, 'Oh, I forgot to tell you—my neighbour, the farmer who lives on the boundary of my property has made an offer to buy the ninety acres from me. Apparently, Mack phoned him and said I was looking for a farmer who would only use the land for agriculture.'

'No, I hadn't heard—but good old Mack. He's such a dear, isn't he?'

Meg gave her a lopsided grin. 'Yes, he's been a good brother, even though he has been a thorn in my side lately. I suppose he has become my rescuer.'

They arrived at the oversized corrugated iron building that resembled an American barn. Meg tried to slide the heavy door open but it wouldn't budge.

'Here—let me have a go.' She moved aside as Jessie pulled and shoved to no avail. 'Have you a piece of wood or something that we can use to push the latch? It appears to have seized up.'

'I know—wait. I've got a heavy screwdriver in my toolkit at the back door.'

Meg returned with her tools. After a bit more wrenching and a great heave from both women, the door opened.

Jessie pinched her nose. 'It stinks of horses in here. You don't have any on the property, do you?' Her eyes squinted from the sun's rays that penetrated the skylight above.

'No, not yet. Wyatt and Joe just rode the quad bikes as Wyatt kept all the pasture for grazing cattle. It must be from Zoro when Mack used to shelter him in here on a cold, winter's night.'

'Well, I think this would be ideal for accommodating children during holiday camps. It's really warm in here and it's in good condition.'

'Where will the ponies go during the winter? This is designed for animals and they'll need shelter during the cold months.'

Jessie appeared to be in deep thought and walked back outside.

Her eyes scanned the estate. 'Where is the boundary of the ten acres you are holding onto?'

'It includes all those paddocks at the rear of the house right up to the treeline by the road and it's all fenced.'

'So that takes in that huge implement shed too. What do you keep in there?'

'It's empty. I've been trying to think of a use for it.'

Jessie's face lit up. 'I've got just the answer! I suggest turning it into an arena with a bunkhouse. You're not still planning on building a swimming pool and tennis court, are you?'

'I was going to do that. Let's go back inside and talk again.'

Once seated in the lounge, they continued their discussion.

'Look, Jessie—I had presumed that Joe would cool down and change his mind. When I last wrote to him, he replied that I was going overboard with the exclusive country lodge idea and the housing development. He doesn't trust me and says that if he comes back, I'll probably start some other hair-raising scheme, and he called me self-centred and ostentatious!'

'Do you love him? If so, maybe ask him what he would like to see happen. That'll be a change from you always having to be in control if you know what I mean.'

Meg walked into the kitchen and left her visitor sitting there. She called out, 'Just putting the kettle on again.'

Jessie sat on the couch trying to make herself comfortable wondering if she overstepped the mark then stood up. 'Don't go to a lot of trouble. Just a cup of that fruit tea I had earlier will be fine—no biscuits for me, thanks.'

Meg lowered a tray with the tea onto the coffee table and sat down. Jessie picked up her cup and returned to the couch.

'Please Jessie ... let's keep chatting ... I've been bottling up all this time and need someone to talk to.' She poured tea for herself from a floral porcelain teapot.

'I know I'll have to give up the idea of the exclusive country lodge. It was my pipedream—but if I want Joe to come back, I'll need to consider his needs too.'

'What does he want to do?'

'He'd rather we did something that would be of service to this community ... I mean ... the land was a gift through the generosity of my family and perhaps we can show charity to others too, he said.'

Jessie leaned over and touched her hand.

'He wanted me to re-evaluate my plans and that's why I agreed to sell to the neighbour.'

'Maybe you have to show him you are doing that. By opening Willow Park as a pony camp, you are giving a service to the community.'

'I think you're right—it's a marvellous idea, Jessie. I'm sure Joe will go along with it. The funds I was going to use for the swimming pool and tennis court can be spent on the arena and the barn accommodation. I'll talk to my builder and get it underway.'

Meg's whole countenance changed. The furrows in her brow became shallower and colour returned to her cheeks. She stood up and wrapped her arms around Jessie.

'That's it! I knew deep down there was another solution to my dilemma. You and Mack have saved me from myself. I can't wait to get my new enterprise started. Oh, and congratulations on your pregnancy. You are going to be the best mother ever!'

'Thanks, Meg—but it's not Mack and me—it's God who is guiding you in the right direction and I think he sent me here to talk to you.'

'I think I'm beginning to realise—but I'm still grateful you put yourself out. You're a kind sister-in-law.'

****

Back at Reed Station, Jessie went into great detail about her visit to Meg and their talk about the pony camp.

Mack placed the last of the dinner plates in the dishrack.

'You're a champion. How did you manage that?'

'I think she was desperate and I arrived just at the right time.'

'It's a great idea of yours, Jessie. It couldn't have come at the worst time as far as availability for us both though. We're going to be too busy to help her on her feet.'

'Hope said she'd give a hand once her baby has settled in. Having children doesn't seem to incapacitate her. I suppose having twins is a bit different but I can help in an advisory capacity I told Meg.'

Mack grabbed the tea-towel out of her hand. 'Let's go and sit down in the lounge. Grandad has turned in already.'

He went in and sat down next to Jessie. She nestled into him.

'I'm going to ask Dad to give her a hand as Hope's father is in demand on their ranch at present. You don't need him around all the time, do you?'

'No, I can spare him at the moment. Now, you need to get your feet up. Bessie left us some of her fruit cake in the fridge—would you like some?'

'No thanks, not at the moment.' She stretched herself out, leaning against Mack. 'I want to make the most of riding Chantilly before the babies come and so I'll take her for a ride tomorrow.'

Mack frowned and looked hard at her growing bump.

'Are you sure it's okay to do that—it won't hurt the babies will it?'

'No, I'll only be walking her and keep close to the tracks. I'll let you know where I'm headed and take a radiophone with me.'

Later in the evening, Jessie stood in front of the bathroom mirror staring at the bulge that had grown twice the size since she had first discovered she was pregnant. She muttered a short prayer before going off to bed.

'Surround these babies with a hedge of protection, God, and help them grow up in the knowledge of you.'

Chapter Twelve

Summer

Willow Park Pony Camp became a great hit in Glenorchy. Children arrived from all around the South Island, many of them bringing their own ponies by horse truck. Meg kept the fees low to include children from families on limited incomes. Mack and Jessie saw a great change in her as she became less self-centred and more focused on how she could help others.

Wyatt and Pru settled into their cottage on Reed Station and Wyatt assisted Meg with the horses a few days a week. She found local volunteers and paid staff to help her run the pony camp.

Great changes took place at Willow Park beginning with the implement barn that was transformed into custom-built rooms with stable doors that opened into simple bunkrooms. These encircled an inside arena, just as Jessie had described to Meg when she'd first suggested pony camp to her.

A few of the regulars to Willow Park were children with special needs. One was a girl with Aspergers called Bonny and the other, a boy with Down's syndrome, called Daniel. They were always accompanied by their carers.

Circumstances meant that Bonny's parents were forced to sell their farmlet which meant the pony, which had been the love of Bonny's life, was taken away. She hated living in the city and became depressed, but with financial aid from the Asperger's

Association, she was able to attend Meg's camps on a regular basis and responded well.

****

This weekend the camp was full. There were children sleeping in the modified barn and those with special needs slept inside the lodge accompanied by their carers. Meg slept inside in the residence and there was Charlie, the caretaker on-site who acted as a security man and lived in the chalet.

On sweltering summer days, the children played in the swimming hole—a natural spring near the main residence which Meg had previously wanted to use for a swimming pool complex.

One evening, when Meg sat in front of her television in her private living room, her solitude was interrupted by pounding at the door.

'Who is it?' she called, reluctant to pull herself away. She was watching a video she'd put on for the evening, sitting back in her armchair with her feet up.

'Sorry, Mrs Wilds,' a timid voice erupted from outside the door. 'Daniel is sickening for something. He's covered in spots and running a temperature. What should I do?'

'Hold on—I'm coming.' She lifted the dinner plate from her lap, gave a loud sigh and hurried into the kitchen. After placing her meal in the warming drawer of her oven, she proceeded to attend to the carer.

Meg took a quick look at Daniel who moaned and kept asking for cold drinks. The red spots on his face and torso looked familiar.

'His sister has recently had chickenpox. Do you think that's what it is?' asked the carer.

'I guess it is. I'm not a medical person but I've worked with a lot of children and I recognise it. You'll have to keep him away from the others and give him plenty of clear fluids.'

She went out to the kitchen and brought back a jug of lemon and barley water. 'Pour Daniel a glass and keep up the fluids. It will help bring his temperature down. I'll phone Doctor Douglas. He's always on call for Pony Camp— it's an agreement we have. I'll be in to see you once I've spoken to him.'

Doctor Douglas took no time at all in arriving at Willow Park which was ten minutes from his home in Glenorchy village. When Meg opened the door to him, a tomato red flush shot up her neck as a radiant smile beamed across his face.

'Oh, Joshua—how nice to see you. Thank you so much for coming after hours. Come this way.' Meg hesitated in front of her hall mirror checking her hair on the way down the passageway. She pulled the loose strands behind her ears.

Meg spoke to Daniel's carer. 'The diagnosis that you and I had deduced was correct. I suppose I'll have to call his parents tonight. It's a pity that they've brought him all the way from Arrowtown.'

'Chickenpox is not serious. He could convalesce here but he'll have to be isolated from the rest of the children as it's highly contagious,' said Joshua.

'I'd better ask his parents to come and collect him.'

'Yes, it's probably best.' His gaze fixed more on Meg's blue eyes than on the boy.

'He'll be so disappointed. He was looking forward to being here,' said his carer.

Meg followed Joshua into the hallway. 'Have you eaten, Joshua? I have a Beef Lasagne I cooked tonight and there's plenty left over.'

'That sounds enticing and I don't have any other house calls, so that is a yes from me.'

Meg phoned Daniel's folks and arranged for them to collect him. 'They'll collect him in the morning,' she said as she sat Joshua down in the lounge. She went to the oven to dish up the food.

'I hope you don't mind eating on a tray on your lap, Joshua. That way, we can sit in front of the television.'

'Not at all—we should do this more often,' he said as he switched on the video they agreed to watch. 'You must come and have dinner with me one evening. Honestly, my cooking won't kill you.' They laughed and sat enjoying the video together for the rest of the evening while now and then Meg checked on Daniel

Her guest's voice was a distant clatter, as she seemed oblivious to his conversation and what she was getting herself into. *He's just a good friend and it beats eating on my own* she kept telling herself.

****

The twins were not due until the end of the month and the intense weight pressing down in Jessie's pelvis caused her to waddle like a duck.

During her pregnancy, she had kept a close bond with Chantilly and decided to give the horse a treat instead of her usual feed. She trudged into the recently built stable-barn and fetched the pellets in a bucket which she carried to the quad bike and placed in the crate. Standing next to the bike, she supported her bulging abdomen with both hands and heaved herself onto the seat. This time, she rode at a snail's pace tensing at every bump along the track to Chantilly's pasture.

The horse was on the far side of the field when she stepped off the bike with the bucket and just as she was about to call out to Chantilly, she let out an almighty, 'Nooooo. Owwww!'

The bucket of feed dropped to the ground and spilt everywhere.

Jessie leaned forward grabbing hold of the wooden gate panting then stumbled back to the quad bike to pick up the radiophone but there was nothing but a crackling sound. The dark storm clouds overhead interfered with the signal.

She groaned once more, holding her belly and slumped onto a hay bale next to the gate.

When she tried the radiophone again it continued to crackle. 'Darn thing! Why don't they make things that work in an emergency?'

She tried to stand but crumbled back onto the hay bale again. 'Please God—let this not be labour pains. I'm far too early and there's nobody around. I don't think I could make it back home on the quad bike.'

She sat with her face in her hands, wondering what she would do if she was in labour and the thought distressed her. She heard a familiar sound and looked up. She was sure she could hear the sound of a horse's hooves pounding the earth.

With all her life-force, she bellowed, 'Help! I'm over here—help me!' Waving her arms in the air.

When she scanned the dirt track, an outline of a black horse began to enlarge and within seconds the animal stood before her with its mount.

'Jessie! What on earth are you doing on the ground? It's getting a bit late in the day for this, isn't it?' Mack had come at the precise moment.

'I've been getting strong cramps in my belly—I hope it's not the babies coming as it's far too early. You'd better call Joshua and get him to come out here pronto and then you'll have to take me back on the quad bike.'

Without a word, he raced over to the gate and led Zoro through into the field. He removed his saddle and bridle and let him loose. 'I'll be back for you, buddy—I've gotta help Jessie first.'

'The horse whinnied and took off across the field.'

****

Back at the homestead, Jessie lay on the bed with Mack sitting next to her.

'Joshua's on his way and I called your mother to ask her to be on standby—just in case. Fortunately for us, your doctor doesn't live too far away.'

'How was it that your arrival was so timely—did you hear me yelling out?'

'No, it had nothing to do with me. It was the same scenario that happened when Grandad collapsed with a stroke in the field when Zoro instinctively knew something was wrong.'

'What do you mean, Zoro?'

'I couldn't control him in the western sector by the old windmill when he got the bit in his mouth, and no matter how hard I tried, I couldn't stop him galloping down the track to you. Somehow he knew you were in trouble.'

'Wow—he's better than a tracker dog. I should have thanked him before you let him loose.'

'It's okay, he'll understand. He has the mind of a human, almost.'

'Owww! Here it goes again. I'm sure I'm going into labour.'

'What can I do for you? Wait... I hear a vehicle.'

Before long, Bessie had the doctor by the arm directing him down the hallway to where Jessie lay.

'Hello there—my goodness, you're a lot bigger than when I saw you last. Has the midwife been to see you recently?'

'Not for a while. I told her I'd decided to stay under your care, seeing you specialise in obstetrics and that you would be delivering my baby.'

'Let me take a look at you.'

Bessie left Jessie and Mack with Joshua.

'You can stay while I examine her if you like. Is that okay Jessie?'

'He can if he wants.' She nodded her head at Mack.

'No, thanks—if you don't mind, I'll just wait at the door. I'll come back in when Joshua has finished, Jessie.'

'Could I please wash my hands?'

'Of course. Follow me.' Mack led him down the hallway to the washbasin in the bathroom.

On his return, the doctor opened his medical bag and took out some instruments, placing them on a clean towel on the side of the bed. Before long, he completed his examination.

'I have finished here. You are in early labour, but it's not critical except you need to be in hospital. Mack—please phone the rescue helicopter. I'll need to talk to the paramedics as your wife will have to be transported to Queenstown Hospital.'

'It's too early for this, isn't it?' Beads of moisture were visible on Mack's forehead.

'Not at all—it's common for babies to be born a few weeks early or late. It's just because twins can offer a few more challenges. Being so isolated out here, it's not the best place for her to be.'

'I see—will she be alright?'

'Everything is perfectly fine and she'll be placed in a facility with all the right equipment.'

'She was hoping for a home birth.'

'That may have been possible with one baby but not with twins, I'm sorry—I did tell her that.'

After Mack had made the phone call, he handed the phone to Joshua who advised the staff about Jessie's condition.

Mack went back into the bedroom to reassure her. 'I'll go with you and I'll phone your folks first to ask for their help. Wyatt could give Grandad a hand on the station and your mother might help get things organised for when we bring the babies home.'

Mack loathed the unwanted panic churning inside him. His chest felt tight when he held his breath in stressful circumstances. He quietly reminded himself to breathe. He sat on the bed caressing Jessie's flaxen, wavy hair.

'Would you like your mother to come with us?'

'No, I need to her to help get the room ready for our babies. She knows what to do—we've already been over it. Is she coming over now?'

'Yes, she said she'll be right over.'

Before the helicopter departed from Reed Station, Pru had arrived and primed her daughter on everything she needed to know and to do once she got to the birthing unit.

'I think it's more important for Mack to be at your side during the birth than your mother. I'll be needed when you bring the twins home and Bessie is looking forward to supporting you too.'

'Thanks, Mum—I'm so glad you're living next door—oh, no—here it comes again. It's getting stronger!'

'Well, the helicopter is just in time then, isn't it?'

Jessie tried to talk between catching her breath with the strong contractions.

Mack packed their bags and gave instructions to Walter about farming agendas for the next few days.

'You can hand most things over to Ben to manage—and make use of Wyatt, Grandad.'

Walter nodded in agreement as he stood next to Bessie on the veranda. They waved them off as Pru drove Jessie and Mack to the helipad in the Land Rover to meet the helicopter. It landed on a field next to the house.

Joshua checked the helicopter that it had everything needed for a birthing emergency and saw them into the air.

He declined an invitation to stay for afternoon tea by Bessie. Before he stepped into his car, he had a quiet word with Mack.

'You have a wonderful sister if I might say so, and she is mighty spunky running that camp by herself. I had an interesting evening with her recently, did she say?'

'Um ... no, she didn't say anything.'

'I had to pay an after-hours visit to a sick child, and she invited me to stay for a meal. A most enjoyable evening and I look forward to paying another visit—if you get my drift.'

Mack was horrified. He didn't think Meg would do something like that—entertaining a male friend so soon after her husband had left the bed. He knew Meg wouldn't do anything to violate her marriage to Joe while they were still working things out, but he was disappointed that she allowed herself to be tempted.

'Please don't be the instigator of more mayhem in my sister's life as she's a married woman to a man she loves. Her life is complicated right now and the last thing she needs is an illicit relationship.'

Joshua leaned on his car with one hand, still holding his medical bag in the other. His face had the appearance of a young child being scolded by a parent.

'I mean no harm—I'm a widower and don't get to spend time with a lovely woman—that's all.'

'It's really none of my business, but I know how impressionable my sister is. Just tread carefully, that's all.'

Joshua kept a leash on his emotions, shook Mack's hand and went on his way.

Chapter Thirteen

December 1983

The twins were born at midnight two weeks before Christmas, a month after Hope Rigby had given birth to a baby girl. Two rowdy, bonny baby boys emerged without complications, one after the other following a long labour. They both had a thick shock of dark hair, like their father.

Jessie lay almost lifeless. The uncharacteristic pallor in her cheeks gave a translucent, deathly appearance. Mack sat at her side holding her hand while the midwife busied herself around him checking her blood pressure and heart rate.

'She needs to rest as there was more blood loss than expected, but it shouldn't impede her recovery. We are monitoring your babies at present, but you will be able to see them before long.'

'Aren't you going to bring them in here?'

'We just have to wait until the paediatrician gives them a full examination as they were under stress during the labour.'

'Oh, I see—will they be alright?' Mack sat wringing his hands while moisture began to form on his temples.

'From my own observation and the comments of the obstetrician, I think they are fine. Don't fret, Mr Reed—you'll see your boys before long.'

Jessie roused, tugging on Mack's coat pocket. 'What's all this about my babies—where are they? I want to have them here next to me.'

The midwife approached her bed. 'Please don't worry, Mrs Reed. Your babies need to spend a short time in the Neo-Natal Unit to be examined by the paediatrician before they can be brought into your room. You all had a bit of a rough time and they're exhausted just like you.'

'Oh, no—I was hoping to start feeding them.'

'You just get some rest. There'll be plenty of time for that and believe me, you're going to need your energy.'

Within a short time, both mother and father closed their eyes and fell asleep. The midwife left Mack lying back in the armchair he had at his disposal next to Jessie and left the room.

****

A week later, the sound of crying babies echoed across the valley at the homestead on Reed Station.

'Breakfast is on the table,' bellowed Bessie down the hallway.

Pru poked her head around the door of the nursery and called back. 'We're almost there, thanks, Bessie. The babies are almost settled.'

Mack came out of the master bedroom in his pyjama pants and headed straight for the bathroom. He washed and returned to the room, stopping at the door of the nursery.

'Thanks so much, Mum for coming over so early each morning to help out. If it wasn't for you, I wouldn't be able to manage the station, honestly.'

'That's okay, Mack. I get a lot of pleasure from this. I'd forgotten what it was like, but it soon came back to me. You get on out there—Wyatt is helping you today, I believe.'

'Yes, I'll make the most of it too. I think he's going to Willow Park next week to help Meg with a few of the ponies that need shoeing. The Blacksmith's going to be there.'

Mack hurried back into the room and within minutes sat with a mug of coffee at the table bolting down the fried eggs and sausages Bessie had put in front of him.

'Jessie shouldn't take long. She's just settling the babies with Mum.'

Bessie sat down at the table and hurriedly ate her own breakfast before the others arrived. 'I've put a lunchbox in your saddlebag at the front door, Mack. I know you're going to be away all day and not home for lunch.'

Mack stood up, wiped the butter from his lips and kissed Bessie on the cheek. 'You're like a mother to me—what would we do without you? Thanks for looking after us all so well.'

Bessie wiped her hands on her apron and beamed at him. 'Go on with you. Stop being so soppy, you big softy.'

Bluey rushed up the steps to meet him as he walked out towards the barn where he kept his quad bikes. The frisky animal jumped on the back while Mack attached the saddlebag taking off along the track in a cloud of dust on this parched summer day.

****

Christmas

Christmas day was a simple affair as everyone was too tired to celebrate in their usual way. The family performed their own church service in the homestead.

Walter dressed in his Sunday best and read from his vintage Bible. They all sang Christmas carols and at the end of the service, the octogenarian prayed for the health and strength of Jessie and her babies.

Mack had invited Meg, but she'd declined to attend and arrived shortly before lunch. He was disappointed that she wasn't ready to join them in giving thanks to God. *What will it take to humble her?* He asked himself.

The family were unable to sit at the table and eat together as they were constantly disrupted by Jessie having to feed the twins on demand.

'Sorry, everyone—just help yourselves. I'll eat after I've put the boys down for a nap.'

Mack could see from the dark shadows under his wife's eyes and her sallow complexion that she was exhausted. 'You aren't doing that on your own—I'll help after you've fed them.'

When they'd finished their meal, Bessie sat next to Pru and Wyatt catching up with all their news.

'Where's Tom?' Bessie asked. 'I hope he's not having Christmas on his own.'

Pru's face took on a sombre expression at the mention of Tom. It was their first Christmas without him.

'No, but he's in good hands—he got engaged recently and his fiancée's parents invited him to join them. He's coming down here for New Year.'

After Jessie finished feeding the babies, she wandered back into the lounge with Mack in tow, each carrying a child. Walter sat back in his chair pensively watching all the comings and goings. The twins were only a few weeks old, and they were the best Christmas present an old man like Walter could ever have. He just couldn't stop staring at them.

'Do you want to hold one of them, Grandad, before they go to sleep? They said at the hospital not to take them out in the community and hand them around to others in case they contract a bug—but apparently, it's okay within the family home.'

While Mack sat with Will, Jessie wrapped Oliver tightly in his delicate woollen shawl that Pru had knitted.

'Just stay there—I'll bring him to you.'

Walter sat holding the child as if the tiny baby was a tinsel ball. He was mesmerised. 'I can't remember what this one is called—in fact, I can't distinguish one from the other yet.'

'That one is called Oliver and his brother is Will. If you look at his nose it's turned up—unlike Will's which is long and narrow.'

'Ah, so they aren't identical twins.'

Mack interjected, 'No, Grandad. We couldn't do that to you. They're going to keep you busy enough without having to work out who's who.'

The baby in his arms relaxed and didn't stir.

Jessie sat next to Meg who didn't appear interested in holding one of the twins.

'How are things going with you, Meg? Is the pony camp working out?'

'Yes, it's going better than I thought. I had a few children with special needs who came to the camp. One child with Aspergers is going to be coming regularly at weekends. Her parents have received a government subsidy as the equine therapy has transformed her so much.'

'Wow, that's great. Perhaps it may be something you could specialise in—equine therapy for children with disabilities.'

'I don't think so— not while I'm alone. I've employed staff but it's not the same as having a husband working alongside me.'

Mack overheard and wanted to say that she shouldn't have chased him away but instead, he kept his mouth shut.

Meg turned to Mack across the room. 'Actually—I want to ask you something, Mack. I remember the story you told me about Zoro being a special horse and that he intuitively knew there was something wrong with Grandad. To add to that, Jessie told me today that Zoro had rescued her when she went into labour. He's an unusual horse and I think he may be able to help this child who has shut down, according to her parents.'

'What child is this,' he asked.

'Bonny—the girl with Aspergers.'

'What do you want Zoro to do?'

'I wondered if you wouldn't mind trucking him over the weekend that Bonny comes to stay next. I'm hoping she can spend time with him, perhaps grooming him and leading him around to see if she can bond with him. I'm sure, by what you've told me, that Zoro can reach her.'

'That's an unusual request but I can see where you're coming from, Sis. I think I could arrange that—when is she coming?'

'At the end of January, during the holidays.'

'It's good you're going to have Mum and Dad stay in the chalet for a while. What time are they arriving?'

Meg looked at her watch. 'They said they'd be here by dinner time around six and I have some food prepared for them. It's a mighty long trip and they'll be exhausted. Mum said they'll be over to visit you all tomorrow.'

Mack looked forward to seeing his parents who were travelling from Nelson. It was going to be a full house, but family life was the one thing that Mack thrived on and he was going to make sure that his boys would grow up in a loving environment.

They were disrupted by Oliver suddenly letting out a roar.

Walter quickly handed him back to Jessie. 'This is where I leave off. I think he's wet and I'll opt-out of that one.'

Jessie and Mack took the babies into the nursery. Within a short time, there was silence. Jessie was finally able to sit down and eat her meal.

It had been a long and tiring day for Bessie. The rest of the family offered to help clean up the kitchen and give her the rest of the afternoon off.

Meg showed her change of heart by washing the dishes and tidying the kitchen before she left to go home. 'Tell Mack that I'll give him a call tomorrow,' she said to her grandfather.

Walter stood up as she walked towards the front door.

'Wait! There's a heap of food in the fridge here. Take some with you. I'll cut some ham and turkey for you. I got extra in with so many people coming and going.'

'Thanks, Grandad. I'll just take a few things to add to my lot. I'll bet Mum has piled the car to the brim with food as usual.'

After Meg left, Pru and Wyatt took their leave and went home. That just left Walter in the lounge alone. He sat back with his berry wine and began to count his blessings.

'Thank you, God, for our beautiful baby boys and this loving family that you have given me. Please keep Len and Helen safe on their long journey to join us so that they can complete the circle.'

Chapter Fourteen

New Year's Eve

Len and Helen settled in at Willow Park and Len spent time during the week tidying up Meg's accounts, although she did have a tax accountant. He wanted to make sure she ran her business efficiently. Helen spent most of her time driving backwards and forwards to Reed Station to spend time with the twins.

'I told Mack we'll be over there again tomorrow,' said Helen. 'I think it would be a good idea for him and Jessie to have some time together tonight. Jessie's brother, Tom has arrived for a few days and she'll want to spend time with him too.'

Helen brought a stoneware pot with a roast chicken to the table with Meg in tow carrying an enamel dish of baked vegetables.

'Yes, I suppose it will be a full house. We could have a quiet evening here, I suppose,' muttered Meg.

Helen started laying the table. 'I expect Jessie will be worn out by the end of the evening with two babies.'

'Where's Dad? Does he know dinner's ready? I'll go outside and get him. I think he has bonded with one of the Kaimanawa ponies from Dart River Ranch.'

Helen winked at Meg. 'That's unusual—he's not into horses much, but perhaps he's softening in his old age.'

'I guess he is,' Meg chuckled as she stood front door where she could see him grooming one of the miniature ponies.

She walked over to him. 'Dinner's ready, Dad.'

He turned around smiling. 'His mane seems to be in a tangle. This one likes me, I think.'

He followed her back to the house. 'Would you like to go for a drive down to the lake with me after dinner? It's such a beautiful day and we could have a bit of father-daughter time.'

'Sure, Dad. We haven't had much time together lately.'

****

After the meal, Len stood ready to take his daughter out for a drive. 'Come on, Meg—we'd better get going so we can make the most of daylight saving. I'll drive if, you like.'

He kissed his wife on the cheek and hurried out to his vehicle parked in the driveway. Helen decided to stay behind to work outside. She'd begun to get friendly with the animals and enjoyed feeding the chickens each evening. In the week she'd been staying with Meg since Christmas Day, she'd planted a garden bed full of petunias and snapdragons and the front yard was an array of bright colours.

While her father drove out to the lake, Meg couldn't stop chatting to him about her pony camp and what she'd done to the property since she'd subdivided it. He pulled in at a rest area beside Lake Wakatipu as the sun faded behind the Humboldt Mountains.

'I'm concerned about you, Meg. You probably don't want me to broach the subject of your marriage, but Joe is a good man and deserves a chance and I think you made it impossible for him.'

Meg went quiet. The corners of her mouth dropped south and the deep crevices returned to her brow. She'd been avoiding any discussion about her marriage during her parents' stay.

'He gave up a lot to give you what you wanted, and you appeared to throw it back in his face. When you lived in Thorndon, he worked hard building a future for you both. He even made a new life in Glenorchy in spite of having never lived in the country before. What's happening now about your marriage?'

Meg opened her passenger window and stared out at the lake. She wouldn't look at her father who continued to shoot sideways glances at her.

'He can come back at any time he likes—it was he who left me, remember? I wrote to him and told him I didn't go through with the housing development and sold the ninety acres as pastoral land to the farmer next door.'

'Was he pleased about that?'

'Yes ... at least I think so. He said I could have left things as they were and shouldn't have considered throwing Wyatt and Pru off the land and out of their home. I don't think he can forgive me for that.'

Meg started sniffing and pulled out a handkerchief and then turned her head away to wipe her wet cheeks with a sleeve.

'It was pretty disruptive for everyone, Meg, but I can see that you are trying to make some drastic changes. Does Joe know all about Willow Park and the pony camp?'

'Yes, I told him in the last letter I wrote. He said it won't be long before I start another impulsive scheme and refers to me as a bull in a china shop.'

'Oh, I see—he still sounds angry. What does he want to do about your marriage?'

'He says he might come down and see what I'm doing after the camp has been running a while.'

'Why don't you start going to church with Mack and Jessie? You could make some new friends there and find some support.'

'I'm fine—thanks, Dad. I have a few friends in the community and the local doctor has offered me support.'

'Oh, really—what kind of support?'

'Mainly with the children when they need medical care, and he plays tennis with me. Joshua is his name and he's a widower.'

'Do you think that's wise if you are trying to mend your marriage?' Len's voice croaked. He coughed to clear his throat.

'We are just friends and I meet all kinds of people through the camp like him. I've made connections with some of the parents who drop their children off here.'

'I suppose you know what you're doing. Just be careful and guard your heart. Single people are vulnerable and you don't need any more complications.'

'Isn't that view marvellous.' Meg pointed at Lake Wakatipu with the mountains in the distance creating an artist's backdrop for a painting.

Len got the message and said no more until they arrived back home.

****

Helen met them at the front door.

'Ah, you're back! Let's sit on the patio and see the New Year in. Bessie gave us a bottle of the award-winning fruit champagne from the Marlborough Sounds. I'll get it out of the fridge.' She took out the bottle while Meg followed her father onto the patio carrying a platter of crackers and assorted cheeses she'd bought at the market.

Helen chatted incessantly while handing around the snacks she'd prepared while they were away.

Len passed Meg the bowl of cashew nuts. 'Isn't it gorgeous down by the lake? I love sitting there staring at the Humboldt Mountains—especially when they are covered in snow.'

'Yes, this place certainly grows on you. I can understand why people want to come and live here.'

'I'm tempted to stay a bit longer, but we have to get back to Nelson. Your father is giving a presentation at the Businessmen's Association there.'

Meg found her tongue. 'I thought you'd retired, Dad.'

'You're right. I need to start pulling back and having fun.'

Helen placed a cheesecake on the table and started slicing it.

'No word from Joe about coming for a visit, Meg?'

'I'll get some plates.' Meg hurried off to the kitchen. When she returned to the patio, she glanced at her mother. 'No—I would have told you if he was coming,' she snapped.

Len darted a disapproving glance at his wife. For the rest of the evening no more was said about Joe and Meg's marriage.

At midnight they all kissed and hugged each other, reiterating the usual *Happy New year* then Len and Helen took themselves off to bed while Meg stayed outside a little longer.

She sat on the patio staring at the neighbour's cows grazing in the paddock next door, illuminated by a full moon. Len and Helen had left her alone, as she appeared to be in another world interrupted by the occasional Morepork in the trees above.

****

Tom was in his element spending January on a high country station. Becoming an uncle to twin boys had also given him much joy as he took turns rocking the babies to sleep when the women weren't fussing over them. Even Walter competed for his share of cuddles and snuggles.

Jessie placed baby Will on the couch to change his nappy. 'When are you going back home, Tom?'

'I can only stay until Tuesday. I've got a shearer arriving with his gang, including a small team of shedhands and I have to be there.'

Jessie finished changing Will and handed him back to Tom.

'It's a pity you couldn't bring Amanda, your fiancée down for New Year.'

'I'll bring her down next time—she's in Australia with her family visiting her brother.'

'That'll be good. Will she be able to the cooking for a gang of shearers when you're married?'

Tom glared at her. 'No, I wouldn't do that to her.' He glanced at Jessie again then saw her winking at Mack and relaxed.

'Where are you getting married? You could always have a ceremony here, can't he Grandad?'

Walter had been nodding off to sleep in his armchair. 'What's that—another wedding?' he stammered.

'Don't worry—Amanda has already arranged it at her own church which we both attend. We're planning the reception garden party on our farm—just like the one you had here.'

Pru came to life all of a sudden. 'Good idea—when will that be?' The woman's eyelids sagged after days of sleepless nights helping Jessie with her night feeds.

Tom looked around for Jessie as the baby began to whine. 'We're not in any hurry—still just thinking about it.'

'That's wonderful, Tom, but don't leave it too long,' she said, winking at him.

Jessie supplemented the hungry babies with milk formula. 'Why don't you top him up with some of this, Tom? I've just warmed it.' She handed him the baby's bottle. 'You can get some practice in as you'll have one of your own one day.'

Pru had been rocking Oliver off to sleep. 'Shall I tuck him into his bassinette?'

'Yes, please. He took all of what I had and some formula so his belly is full,' said Jessie.

'Have we been keeping you up, Grandad?' Jessie teased Walter. 'I hope you think it's all worthwhile having us living here with you.'

Walter pulled himself together. He stood up and tousled Jessie's hair. 'I couldn't think of any other way to spend my old age, my girl. This is more than I could hope for.'

'I'm going to put the kettle on if anyone wants a cuppa.' He wandered through to the kitchen.

Wyatt sat chatting with his son until Walter arrived back in the lounge with the teapot and cups on a tray. 'Help yourself, everyone.'

'Tom and I are taking up your offer of spending tomorrow working with you on the station, Mack.'

'Thanks a lot. It's going to be a hectic day—we have shearers arriving and need to bring the young hoggets off the hills to the woolshed for crutching to prevent flystrike. We have shepherds, of course, and the dogs do the work—but I'm talking about thousands of sheep.'

'Wow, that's a lot of sheep compared to our farm,' Tom said, glancing at his father.

'Yep, sure is. That's not counting Mack's three Angus bulls and two hundred Angus heifers.'

Tom rubbed his hands together. 'It'll be a terrific experience.'

'You're right, son. It's going to be an eye-opener for you. Mack's going to give shearing training to students from Lincoln University Summer School at the end of the day. He has won several Golden Shears awards and will show you some good tips.'

It was a hive of activity on Reed Station. Not only were there second and third-generation, Reed family shepherds but in Jessie's family there were also second and third-generation shepherds too. And now they were one big blended family. What more could a man ask for? Thought Mack as he helped himself to tea after offering his wife a cup.

Chapter Fifteen

Mack was relieved that the hectic Christmas and New Year period was over. The family had all dispersed and returned to their home towns. He and Jessie relished the quietness in the house and Pru had left them to it, as she was eager to get back to her own bed.

The day had come for Mack to take Zoro to pony camp for Bonny to ride. He and Meg had promised her this and they wanted to give her a real farming experience seeing that most of her depression had been as a result of her family leaving the country for the city and selling her pony.

Zoro grazed in the large paddock near the stables. He came trotting towards the gate with both ears pricked forward when Mack ambled up to the fence.

The horse licked his hand. 'Hi, fella.' Mack opened the gate and approached him with a halter. 'We're going for a ride in the horse truck today as you've got some special work to do.'

He slipped his headcollar on and then his bridle on top fastening the cheek strap. It was as though Zoro knew he was on a special assignment as he nudged his owner affectionately. After he'd tacked up, he rode bareback down the track to the stable-barn to fetch his saddle. While Zoro was tied to the hitching rail, Mack carried the saddle to the horse truck. Within a short time, he had loaded Zoro and headed off to Willow Park.

He arrived to find cars blocking the driveway, preventing him from driving the truck through to the trailer park. As he pulled up behind the cars, Meg came around the side of the house to greet him. He rolled down his window. 'Can you ask these people to shift their vehicles? I have a horse in the truck.'

'Sorry, Mack. I forgot to let them know you'd be coming with Zoro. I'll get them to shift right now. If you put Zoro in the stable next to Toby, I'd like to tell you about Bonny. Her mother has just been and gone and I've had an update.'

Mack's eyes narrowed. 'I'll drive down next to the stables once this car gets out of my way.' He tried not to sound pushy but it irritated him that people could be so inconsiderate.

Once he was able to drive the truck down to the stables, he took Zoro out and led him into the barn next to Toby, a white pony that was docile around other males. He went inside the house to find Meg had made a pot of tea and to his unbelief, fresh scones.

'You didn't bake these, did you?'

'No, I cheated. Mum made a huge batch before she left after New Year. I keep them frozen and just heat them before serving.'

The scones were dripping in strawberry jam and fresh cream from the neighbour's cows.

'These are good—thanks, Mum,' he said facetiously, winking at Meg while catching a drip of cream on the end of his chin.

'I'm glad of a bit of a catch up with you. Have you heard from Joe—is he coming back?'

Meg's face dropped. 'I wish everyone would stop badgering me about him. I don't know what he's going to do,' she growled.

'Oh—sorry, Sis. I'm just concerned, that's all. By the way—my mate, Tony from Federated Farmers said he saw you and that new doctor fella—what's his name? He saw you having lunch with him down by the lake the other day.'

Meg put her teacup down. It clanged, almost breaking. She stammered, 'That's right, he's giving me advice and support while working with clients with special needs and has made a few house calls lately to the children.'

'Look ... I don't want to interfere, but I hope you know what you're doing. When Jessie and I came to see you that day, you said you love Joe and that you want him back—so please be careful.'

'Didn't you come here to talk about how Zoro is going to help Bonny?'

'Sure—tell me all about her.'

'Bonny has Asperger Syndrome and when her family moved from Arrowtown to live in Queenstown, she began to suffer from depression after her parents made her give up her pony when they moved to the city. The horse was her best friend, her comforter.'

Mack lowered his eyebrows, creating wrinkles in his forehead. 'Really? That's pretty harsh for a young girl.'

'She comes here to ride on a regular basis. Now that Christmas is over, she'll start coming back more often.'

There was a knock at the door. 'Come in!' Meg called out.

'Sorry to interrupt you, Mrs Wilds. We are ready to start the children in the arena. Should we wait for you?'

'Thanks, Sara. No—tell the staff to just carry on as usual. I need to sort something out for Bonny. Is she still sitting under the umbrella out there?'

'Yes—she's waiting for a visitor.'

Meg gave her a nod. 'Tell her I'll be out soon.'

'I'd better wind this up and get out there. I'd like to get Bonny handling Zoro then perhaps she can ride him tomorrow morning. I want her to do the whole thing while you're here, such as grooming, fastening a blanket, feeding, and then leading him around. If you can spare Zoro until tomorrow afternoon, I'll go over tacking with her and some of the others after you've taken Zoro back to the station. She's going home on Monday evening.'

'I can give you today and tomorrow morning, but you'll have to work with her yourself after that. I'll stay here tonight and then I'll have to leave tomorrow afternoon.'

'That's okay. I have some great volunteers for the long weekend along with a few paid staff and most of them are experienced.'

Mack walked over to introduce himself to Bonny. Her face lit up instantly. 'Come with us, Bonny to see a friend in the stable who wants to meet you.' Mack directed her to the stable where Zoro waited and as she approached, the stallion let out a soft whinny.

When the girl draped herself over the wooden rail, the horse licked her hand. 'Hello, Zoro—my name's Bonny. Mack said you're my new friend.'

Mack held up a bucket. 'Here, Bonny, give him some of these pellets. Put them into the palm of your hand and let him take them.' Meg stood alongside her.

While the horse nibbled on the pellets in her hand, Bonny let out a squeal. 'Ooh—that tickles,' she squealed.

'He loves you already, Bonny. Now I want you to give him a good brush. You know what to do—the grooming kit is over there in the box.'

Meg turned to Mack who leaned over the hitching rail listening and observing.

'I try to foster independence in the children, as many of the children have *learned helplessness* and this training enables them to become self-reliant.'

This whole new side to his sister impressed Mack. She had trained as an occupational therapist for children with developmental delays and had given it up to join their father's import business and had been a hard-nosed businesswoman.

'He's a big horse, isn't he? I think he likes me and I love him,' Bonny blurted.

By the afternoon, with her head in the air, Bonny led Zoro around the enclosed arena. The girl was tall for her age which made the towering, black horse less intimidating.

Mack fastened the reins to the saddle and asked Bonny to walk around the arena and back again without leading the horse. As she did this, Zoro sauntered behind her and wherever she turned, he followed.

For the rest of the afternoon, Mack and Meg watched as Bonny lunged Zoro in the arena, and by the end of the day, she had won him over. The horse trusted her.

'Please, Mrs Wilds. Can I have Zoro every time I come here?'

'We'll see, Bonny—I'll do my best, but this is Mack's stock horse and he might need him.'

'Maybe Bonny might like to pay Zoro a visit to Reed Station one weekend. If you or someone can drop her off, I can bring her back to you at the end of the day,' said Mack, tousling Bonny's hair.

'Good idea, brother. You're right about this horse being special.'

They watched as Bonny groomed Zoro who rubbed his head up and down her back and then licked her hand.

'Oooh,' she squealed. 'You made my hand all slimy, Zoro.'

Meg slipped her hand in her pocket. 'Here, Bonny. Give him this apple and he'll love you forever.'

The stallion behaved perfectly with Bonny. They had made friends for life.

Mack stayed overnight in one of Meg's spare rooms. He wanted to make sure Zoro was going to be on his best behaviour and didn't want to leave Meg to handle him on her own, as she wasn't used to him.

When they had finished cleaning up after the evening meal, the children went to their respective bedrooms—some sleeping in the barn on the hay bales, a few in the lodge and the rest in the arena bunkhouse.

Later that evening, Mack sat with his sister enjoying homemade lemonade and crackers with fresh goat cheese from her neighbour.

'Oh, no. Who's disturbing us at this hour? It's rare that I can have an evening's rest without some kind of interruption.'

The knock on the lounge door became louder. Meg hauled herself up off the sofa and opened the door.

'What is it, Carrie—it's getting late?'

A girl no older than sixteen stood wrenching her hands behind her back.

'Sorry, Mrs Wilds—it's Bonny—she's gone.'

Meg's mouth dropped open. Her brows raised.

'What ... what do you mean, gone? Why isn't she in the room with you?'

'I thought she was asleep. I had dozed off and when I got up to go to the bathroom, her bed was empty.'

'Oh, no! Mack—help me find her!'

She turned to the young girl. 'Carrie, don't worry. She has probably gone outside because she couldn't sleep. Go back to your room. We'll find her.'

Meg tugged Mack's sleeve. 'I'll grab a torch. Wait for me out the front.'

Mack went to his room, pulled on his Swanndri jacket and waited on the front porch for her. From there he could see a dull light emanating from the stables. *That's strange. There shouldn't be anyone out there at this time.*

Meg joined him. 'I've got the torch, but the battery is weak and it might not last.'

'Look over there.' He pointed in the direction of the stables. 'You didn't leave the night light on in there, did you?'

The corners of her eyes wrinkled as she tried to determine what the light was. 'No, I didn't. It is never left on unless we have a sick animal.'

'Come on, let's check it out—but first, you wait here while I take a look in the horse trailer park to see if there is a strange vehicle there.'

Mack shot off with the torch before Meg could reply. She shivered as she wrapped her arms around herself, watching the ghostlike silhouettes of branches catch the half-moon beams as they swayed in the breeze

'Ah! Don't creep up behind me like that!' Meg scolded as Mack arrived back at her side in a short time.

'Shhh—keep your voice down.'

'Did you see any vehicles?'

'Nothing.' Mack heard the chattering of teeth as she spoke.

'Cold are you? Here, I've got a jumper on under this. You never seem to dress warmly.' He pulled off his jacket and handed it to her.

'Okay, brother—no need to lecture me.' She sniffed at the jacket, screwed up her nose and pulled it on. 'Where to now?'

'Follow me and not a whisper. Let's catch the culprit.'

Meg held on to the hem of his jacket as she tiptoed furtively behind him.

'Just wait here, Meg. For all we know they might have a weapon.'

'Listen.' She put her hand up to his chest to stall him. 'I hear the sound of hooves. They're in the process of stealing one of my ponies. How can they if they've no horse trailer? Maybe it's parked down the road, or worst still, they intend to steal yours.'

'I'll stop them. You get ready to go inside the house to call the police when I say.'

Mack crept up to the side of the barn. He edged his way to the open doorway and poked his head inside then stopped short, staring in disbelief. It was as if he was hallucinating. There was a young girl wearing white pyjamas riding Zoro around the arena bareback. He lurched forward then stalled, not wanting to alarm her.

Zoro began walking towards him.

'Halt, Zoro. You're going the wrong way,' the girl commanded then looked over in Mack's direction. She froze when she spotted him and pulled on the rope she'd attached to Zoro's halter.

Mack approached his horse and took hold of his halter. By this time Meg had entered the barn.

'What's all this about, eh? Why are you out here?' Mack helped her climb down then Meg took her by the hand and led her away to the side. The girl appeared so stunned to be caught in the act that she couldn't find the words to say to her accusers.

Mack put Zoro back in his stall and placed some hay in his hanging feeder. He unclipped his rope and hung it back on the hook before joining Meg and Bonny.

'You don't know how worried we've been. We thought you had gone missing and were about to call the police. What were you doing?'

Bonny lowered her head then her brown, marble eyes misted over. 'Sorry, Mrs Wilds. I couldn't sleep until I'd ridden Zoro. He loves me and I wanted to keep him company out here. It's not his home and I thought he would be lonely.'

Meg put her arm around Bonny.

Mack's eyes twinkled as he beamed at her. 'He must love you a great deal to let you ride him around the arena with only a halter.'

Meg directed her towards the door. 'Come on, missy. Time for you to get to bed. Perhaps Mack will let you ride Zoro tomorrow, but we need to see you using a saddle and bridle first.'

Bonny looked directly at Mack. 'Please, Mr Mack—let me ride Zoro tomorrow. I have to go home on Monday and I won't see him for ages.'

Meg whispered in Mack's ear. 'Zoro is a lot taller than the pony she once owned.'

'Of course, Bonny, but I need to go over a few things with you on how to handle him first,' Mack replied. 'We'll do that in the morning.'

****

Mack spent the next day with Bonny showing her how to tack up Zoro on her own and by the afternoon, she was well on her way trotting and cantering in the arena. The horse connected with the girl in an uncanny way, Mack thought. *Zoro really is something special. I knew I'd chosen a unique horse.*

'I can't wait to come back next time. Please let me look after him again,' Bonny pleaded.

Mack patted her on the back. 'We'll check with your folks if you can visit us at Reed Station next time you come. Zoro will be waiting to see you.' She dashed over to Zoro's side and threw her arms around his neck before Mack led him to the horse truck.

Meg stood next to Bonny as Mack drove off with Zoro down the long driveway and out onto the main road. He tooted, as he drove past the farm and he could see Bonny still waving in the distance on the front veranda of the house. Mack knew he and Zoro had helped to heal a broken heart.

****

Jessie managed the twins with occasional assistance from her mother, Pru who helped mostly by bringing meals that she could put in the freezer. Jessie had organised the on-call vet to fill in for her for while she was on maternity leave, but she was determined to get back to work once she could leave the babies with their grandmother—even if it was only part-time.

Jessie held Oliver in one arm and pulled back the curtain at the window when she heard Mack's truck revving next to the stable-barn. She grinned at her mother who was busy burping Will.

'Ah, good—he's just in time to help me bath the twins.'

She walked over to the window and pulled back the curtain. 'He's just unloading Zoro now.'

'Poor man. He'll be tired out, won't he? I can give you a hand to bath them.'

'No, Mum. It's good for the boys to get used to both of us handling them. We share roles in this household and I herded cattle on horseback before I fell pregnant while trying to run my veterinary business. We are equals in this marriage.'

Pru gave her a half-smile as she took a pillow-case from the pile of washing in the wash basket and started folding it after sniffing at it first. 'The washing smells so fresh after hanging in the sun with the breeze we've had today.'

A thud resounded from heavy boots climbing the veranda steps. Mack left them at the door and walked inside baring his thick, woollen socks.

'Ah! My boys are still up. Not bathed yet?'

'No, Dad—they're waiting for you and you're just in time.' Jessie lifted her head pursing her lips, waiting for Mack to kiss her. He leaned over and planted one on her mouth.

'I won't touch the babies until I clean up. Won't be long and then I'll help give them a bath.' Mack shot into the bedroom and then into the bathroom with fresh clothes in his hands.

After his shower, he arrived to assist with bath time. Once it was over, Jessie was eager to get the babies settled in their bassinettes and off to sleep. This evening, they went down without a fuss and the house was quiet again.

Jessie massaged her neck muscles. 'What a relief—it has been a long and tiring day. Oliver had colic all morning. It must have been something I've eaten. Maybe too much garlic in that chicken hotpot last night.'

'Well, you'd better not tell Bessie that. It's one of her mother's recipes. She's a bit sensitive when it comes to critiquing her cooking.' Mack knew that from past experience.

'How about you, Mack—how did it go with Bonny—did she take to Zoro okay?'

'It was more than Meg and I could hope for. The girl and Zoro are like old friends. She took off outside last night to the stables and unhitched Zoro. After jumping on him bareback she walked him in circles around the arena in her pyjamas. Meg and I thought we had intruders in the barn when we spotted a dim light coming from there and were about to call the police. When we discovered her, we were so amazed at the sight of the two of them bonding we couldn't get angry at her.'

'Wow. What a story—it sounds unreal.'

'Remember when you found Zoro with Grandad when he collapsed in the field following his stroke? Zoro covered him with hay from the bale at the gate to keep him warm. You said he had extra-sensory perception and I think you're right.'

'Yes, and he also rescued me on the dirt track when I went into early labour.'

'You also said that one day he'll be able to help others to heal and it's already happening. Bonny is going to pay us a visit in a few weeks' time. She'll stay at Willow Park but she can come out here for a ride on the station during mustering.'

'I can't believe Meg is making provision for all this and I never thought she'd go down this track. If only Joe could see her now.'

'She doesn't seem to want to talk about him. I'm afraid that doctor of yours has turned her head and I hope she isn't on course for another disaster. I tried to warn her off him.'

Jessie lay back on the couch with her head on Mack's lap. He played with her hair, twisting it around his finger. 'I'll keep praying that the Lord will give her wisdom and a desire for her marriage to be restored,' he said as Jessie closed her eyes while Mack chatted incessantly about the pony camp. His voice seemed to lull her to sleep. He got up and looked around the room, spotting a woollen rug on an armchair. After he draped it over her, he kissed her forehead and turned out the light.

Chapter Sixteen

Autumn

Mack had been up since five bringing the sheep off the hills with the musterers and driving them into the holding pens at the woolshed. They were on horseback except on the steeper hills where it would be lethal to go by horse—then they went by foot climbing the craggy hills with their dogs and a shepherd's crook.

This year, the shearing gang brought their own shedhands and cooks. Bessie and her domestic staff usually cooked all the meals, but now things had changed, she didn't mind at all. Mack left the shearing gang in the hands of his trusty Head Shepherd, Ben.

The drought conditions on Reed Station had taken its toll. Mack guided Zoro up the track onto the jagged ridge overlooking the farm. As far as he could see around him, the high country gave a scorched appearance as though a fire had seared the terrain. The yellow-brown colour was characteristic of the Otago district, the land of extremes—parched summers and chilling, icy winters. As he looked around at the desert landscape, he could see the damage the drought had done to the hillsides.

Although they had suffered a summer drought, by God's grace the autumn rain had allowed a little grass to grow and provided extra feed for the animals. Mack and his shepherds had checked the sheep for facial eczema early that morning and there was no sign of it, although there was always a risk after a warm rain.

He was grateful the station had a fresh water supply for the animals from a few streams that crossed the land, fed by the pristine glacial waters.

Mack gave Zoro his head as the horse reached down to graze on random blades of grass he could forage at his feet. His rider sat upright, breathing in the chilly, late afternoon air which caught his breath as he exhaled.

Awe transformed his face. He squinted through the sun's glare as he peered at the panoramic spectacle before him that reached as far as he could see. The vastness of the station astonished him as his eyes welled up knowing how blessed he was to have the responsibility of managing a high country station.

Something heavy hit his stomach causing him to grimace. Did his guilt of giving Meg his own small estate still linger? He was only trying to counterbalance the two-thousand-acre station he'd inherited from his grandfather—and look at the chaos it had caused. Life was so good for him right now—a far cry from that of his sister for whom he began to have empathy. Meg's life was hanging in the balance.

Zoro flinched. 'Whoa, boy—what's up?' Mack pulled him up on a short rein as a hawk flew out from behind a towering rock and startled him.

'Come on, fella, we'd best be going back.'

He eased Zoro down the narrow track that led off the ridge into the valley. Each step the horse took he calculated on the rugged, steep hillsides. Mack recalled the time he'd received the news that a neighbouring stockman died when his horse slipped and fell, crushing him to death. He shivered at the memory. Such freak accidents like that don't happen often, but they do occur—one of the many hazards of life on a high country station and he was determined they weren't going to happen under his management.

As he glanced towards the west, the rusty, iron roof of a musterers' hut caught his attention. He would have to get it repaired. Next, he had to check the winter crops on that side of the station.

He edged his way down, urging Zoro on towards the feed shed to check the winter supplies before heading home. The gate to the paddock was already open as there was no stock on this corner of the station. The stockmen had moved them earlier in the week.

When they arrived at the shed, Mack gave Zoro a long rein to let him eat remnants of hay which lay on the ground. When he looked inside the shed his heart sank. The stock levels were at an all-time low as hay and silage were hard to source in the province.

Mack pulled on the reins to let Zoro know that his snack-time was over. He turned to head home, gazing at the extensive paddocks before him when abruptly his face changed. Something caused his eyes to sparkle and lift his spirit—it was the tender, young grass that formed a lush carpet contrasting with the bronze hills. *Thank you, God! New grass for the stock.*

He let Zoro lower his head as the animal craned his neck towards the new grass.

'Mmm. This is a blessing, Zoro, my boy. It's a good sign and so early in the year too.'

He always chatted to Zoro, like other farmers in the area, who were accustomed to talking to their working dogs or themselves in these isolated areas. Out there, these faithful friends could often be the only companionship shepherds and stockmen enjoyed—especially when they spent days in the saddle staying overnight in cold, wooden huts.

Walter had worked hard providing feed for the stock before Mack arrived at the station. When his grandfather was fitter and younger, he'd toiled maintaining crops of swedes and turnips with the help of young labourers—most of whom were horticultural students from Lincoln University. Now that the old man was unable to tend the land, Mack had employed a married couple to manage the crops.

As Zoro trotted at a slow gait towards the fields of winter feed boasting row upon row of green tops, a man and woman in matching denim overalls waved out. Pete, the supervisor turned around and spoke to the workers then walked over to greet Mack, while Pete's wife, Kathleen carried on working alongside the others.

'Hi there. Haven't seen you around for a while. How is it all going?' He removed his hat to scratch his head then pushed it back on his head.

'The twins keep us busy when I'm not out here—life's hectic right now.' He pointed at the ground. 'The crops are flourishing.'

'They sure are. Must be the warm rain we've been getting. It's mild for April. I hope it keeps up so we can have plenty of feed before the winter sets in. We're trialling kale next week.'

'Well done—we're getting low on feed, so hopefully they'll be ready in time. I don't want to have to buy another load of silage right now. By the way—you and Kathleen must visit and see the twins. Give Jessie a call soon as she'd love to see you both. She hasn't seen you since the wedding.'

'We sure will. I'd best be getting on as we've got a bit to do before dark.' He was about to walk off when he stopped short.

'Wait ... how did you get on in the Golden Shears contest this year? Did you win this time?'

'I couldn't get away this year—not with Jessie having twins. I was happy enough with second place last year, but if all the goings-on here hadn't distracted me, I could have won—sorry, I'd best be getting on now too.'

Mack waved out to Kathleen as Pete walked back to join her and the other gardeners.

It was late in the afternoon. The sun began to disappear behind the towering hills earlier in Dart Valley and it was time to get back and give Jessie a hand with the babies. As he rode out onto the dirt track, he was about to break into a canter when he thought he could see someone on horseback waving to him in the distance.

Who could that be? The stockmen wouldn't have a reason to be riding over this side of the station. At least, not at this time of the year.

As the person rode closer, the sun rays outlined the silhouette of golden hair willowing in the breeze under a Stetson. The horse had been in a shadow but now it was evident it was Chantilly. Jessie waved out as she came closer. When she met up with Mack, a wide grin stretched across her face.

'What brings you here—who's looking after the twins?'

'Mum is clucking over them as usual. They aren't feeding so often now and I can get away between feeds. I just had to experience the elements and spend some time with Chantilly. I want to enter her in the Agricultural and Pastoral Show next spring. She does dressage so well.'

Mack was so glad he'd given Chantilly to Jessie for a Christmas present the year he'd proposed to her. She and the horse had bonded more than Mack had expected. They were inseparable.

'I'm glad to see you're getting back into riding. I think Chantilly has missed you—but please, be careful not to overdo it. You'll burn out and that won't be any good. You said you're wanting to return to work after you wean the boys.'

Mack caught himself. He knew he had a tendency to be over-protective of Jessie who didn't appreciate it. He wished he'd kept his mouth shut.

'I'll know when I'm doing too much. I'm fine—really. Let's canter down the track—coming?'

Mack breathed a sigh of relief that she didn't take exception to his comment, however caring he'd intended it.

They headed off towards the far end of the paddock. Mack slid off Zoro to open the gate and let Chantilly through.

'Thanks! I catch you back at the stables.'

Jessie took off in a flash with Zoro in close pursuit cantering along the track, creating billows of dust and gravel behind them. Mack pulled back when he started eating dirt and let her go.

As they rode towards the stables, Pru stood waving from the veranda, holding one of the babies. They took care of the horses and hurried to the homestead.

'What's up, Mum?' Jessie asked, still panting.

'This little minx wouldn't go down to sleep after his last feed. He must have known you had gone.'

Mack and Jessie removed their boots and followed Pru inside.

'Sorry, Mum—I wasn't really that long. I'll just wash my hands and take him from you.'

Jessie went off to the bathroom while Mack disappeared out the back. She returned at once and took Will from her mother's arms.

'I'll try to put him down. You go off home, Mum. Dad will be thinking you have deserted him. Thanks so much for today.' She leaned over and kissed her on the cheek.

'My pleasure, my dear. Dad's taking me into Glenorchy tomorrow for lunch and to get some groceries. I'd really like to go to Queenstown but I'll leave it for another week.'

'Before you go, I'll give you a list of a few items I need at the store if you don't mind.'

'That's fine. Have a good night.'

Mack returned from washing up and walked her to the door.

'Thanks for everything, Mum. You know we are both very grateful for all the help you give us. Take a break tomorrow. I've got the afternoon off and can give Jessie a hand with the boys.'

Chapter Seventeen

Wyatt was proud of his new pickup. It was bright red, similar to Cole Rigby's Chevrolet—a late model Ford and it was something he'd promised himself when he retired, he'd once told Mack.

As he pulled in next to their cottage, Pru caught sight of Mack returning from the cattle yards on Zoro and waved out to him. He'd been on the north side of the station working with the stockmen on horseback since dawn. They brought down the herd of young Angus steers from the foothills ready for the stock trucks to collect early the next day. He'd just finished giving them a feed of hay.

'Mack! Join us for a coffee if you've got time. We need to talk to you about something,' said Pru as she stepped out of the vehicle.

'I've got some of that milk stout in the fridge if you want one,' said Wyatt as he reached into the vehicle to help Pru carry the boxes of supplies from the General Store.

'Sure, will do—but I can't stay long. I promised Jessie I'd help with the boys this afternoon and I'm running late.'

Mack followed them both inside. He smiled and nodded as he viewed the new curtains and fresh paint. They'd both been busy renovating the cottage.

Wyatt handed Mack the stout. 'It's not really beer, is it? My folks have drunk it for years and said it was medicinal. I suppose I got into it through them,' said Wyatt.

Mack took a seat. 'Yes, it's great. Grandad introduced me to it. I'm also partial to homemade apple cider if it's not too strong.'

'Well, we'd better get to the point,' said Pru, elbowing Wyatt who sat next to her on the couch.

'When we drove towards Glenorchy this morning, we caught sight of Joe driving an Avis rental car, and he appeared to be heading out of town towards Willow Park. When we left the General Store, we took a drive down by the lake before we had lunch at that little cafe.' Pru looked at her husband. 'You tell them, dear.'

Wyatt hesitated then finished telling the story.

'I took some photos of the lake to send to Tom as he wants to show them to his girlfriend. The strange thing is—as we pulled out of the carpark, we saw Meg sitting on the park bench with Dr Douglas, both wearing tennis outfits and so I just kept driving. I know that she and the doctor are good friends.'

Pru interjected. 'I don't think Meg expected a visit from Joe. Perhaps he was going to give her a surprise visit.'

Mack raised his eyebrows. 'You're right—I spoke to Meg on the phone yesterday and she didn't say anything about Joe coming to visit.'

He took hold of his Stetson he'd placed on the seat next to him and rushed down the rest of his stout. 'It doesn't sound good to me. I'm sorry, but do you mind if I head off home? I'd better ask the family if Joe has called by or phoned while I was out.'

Mack rushed to the door with the couple in tow.

'Thanks for letting me know … oh, and thanks for the stout. It's a good brew. I'll let you know if we hear from either Joe or Meg.'

****

Mack and Jessie had no sooner settled the twins down for their afternoon sleep than the sound of a vehicle's engine whirred in the driveway. Mack had already told Jessie about the chain of events that Pru and Wyatt had witnessed. Could this be Joe on their doorstep?

The vigorous pounding on the door echoed down the hallway. Jessie got up and peered through the Venetian blinds.

'Oh no, it's Joe, sure enough—and he appears pretty agitated. Answer the door, quick, Mack before he wakes the boys. It doesn't sound good.' She raked her hair with her fingers, pushing it back behind her ears.

Mack opened the door to Joe whose eye sockets revealed large dark rings shadowing intense, soulful eyes. He looked at Mack with relief as he stood in the doorway.

'Thanks, mate. Do you mind if I come in? Something is going on with Meg.'

Mack took his arm and led him into the lounge then Jessie stood up and greeted him with a hug. 'I'll put the kettle on,' she said, sensing the need to remove herself.

Within a short time, she returned with a tray of tea and biscuits. Moving quietly around the lounge, she placed the tray on the side table.

'Tea, Joe?'

'Please,' he answered with a shaky voice.

''I remember how you like it.' Jessie poured three cups of tea and sat down while Mack passed the biscuits around.

'Thanks, Jessie—please come and join us. I'd like your input too if you don't mind.'

Mack couldn't help noticing how thin Joe had become since moving back to Wellington. He had always been a tall, lean man but this time he looked scrawny. Even his fingers appeared to be white, raw-boned twigs.

'Gee whiz, Joe. What've they been feeding you in Wellington? You could do with a good feed.'

'Yeah, well ... all this drama with my wife isn't exactly conducive to healthy living.'

Mack flashed a glance at Jessie and began kneading his neck muscles. 'I thought she may have settled down by now as we have seen she has made major changes.'

'You can say that again! You mean by changing husbands. She has hardly let the grass grow under her feet, that's for sure.'

Mack thought he would make sure they were both on the same page before he made any comment.

'Do you mind explaining why you are here? I mean ... what has upset you so much ... have you been to see Meg?'

Mack made sure he wasn't going to be the one to drop the bombshell. It would come from Meg. She could at least have the integrity to tell him herself.

'I've just passed through the town and stopped to buy Meg a small box of those *Roses* chocolates she likes from the General Store. As I walked towards my car, I saw a man and a woman in tennis clothes drinking milkshakes. I almost dropped the chocolates when I thought I recognised the woman from behind and then I heard a familiar giggle. It was Meg, and she appeared to be flirting with this fellow. I ducked behind my vehicle until they were further along the road and watched them cross to the other side and get into the car. I saw the vehicle veer off and turn down the road towards the lake.'

Joe's eyes began to mist over. He squeezed his eyes shut a few times as if to blink back the tears then he wiped his face with the back of his hand.

Mack tried to quell the anger rising within him and whispered to Joe. 'What did you do then?'

'I confess I just couldn't help myself as I had to get at the truth. There was an empty carpark in the church where I could wait unseen. It was a place to hide until they had reached the lake in their vehicle then I walked towards the lake.'

This is beginning to sound like a thriller, Mack thought, while Jessie remained quiet, allowing Joe to offload on his brother-in-law.

Joe gulped down the last of his tea. He coughed as though he was choking. 'Sorry—went down the wrong way.' He cleared his throat. 'I probably could have done with something stronger if I wasn't driving.'

'Sorry, Joe, but we don't have anything in the house.'

He continued. 'I couldn't believe my eyes. When I approached their park bench next to the lake, the two appeared to be real palsy-walsy from where I was standing behind the large oak tree.'

For the first time, Jessie spoke up. 'They weren't kissing though, were they?'

'No, not kissing. They were eating sandwiches together. Their obvious fraternising is enough for me to know it's time to quit.'

Jessie asserted herself, 'I think they're just good friends and companionship fills a need for them both right now. I'm sure that's as far as it goes.'

'How do you know that and how long has it been going on?' Joe's face reddened as the heat of his anger ensued.

Mack began to sense Joe's exasperation. Was he deflecting blame for his wife's indiscretion onto him for not disclosing her secret life? Even though she'd not been covert about her relationship with the doctor in Glenorchy, she'd kept it from Joe. Perhaps he should have made more of an effort to return to his wife. Mack began to see it was time to challenge Joe about his own behaviour.

'Listen, Joe. I understand you're angry and disappointed with Meg, but hear me out as there are always two sides to a story.'

'You mean three sides! Fair enough.' Joe slumped forward on his chair and leaned on his knees, half glaring at Mack, looking down at his feet. His mouth curved downwards as his forehead puckered.

Mack spoke with an air of authority. 'I've spent much time with Meg analysing where she is at with your marriage. It's really not our business, but she has involved Jessie and me on several occasions making it clear she does love you and seeks the restoration of your marriage. After numerous rebuffs when she urged you to return, she just gave up.'

Joe lifted his head and sat upright eyeballing Mack.

'What are you trying to say—that she doesn't want me back now?' He sat there with eyes wide, licking his bottom lip.

'No, I'm not saying that at all. She had turned her life around in many ways, but when you refused to return to her, temptation set in. The doctor is a lonely widower and Meg is all alone on that large estate by herself, apart from the caretaker, Charlie who keeps to himself. If you work on it right now, you may be in time to save your marriage—though I'm not sure—you'll have to do some convincing and hear her out.'

'I ... I'm not sure what to think. She didn't waste any time finding a replacement. I might need to go away and think about it, but thanks for letting me know. I'll get off now and look for some accommodation.' He picked up his car keys and rattled them.

'Thanks for the tea, Jessie.'

As he walked to the door, Mack jumped up quickly. 'Wait! Why don't you stay for a while—have some dinner with us later? You haven't given me a chance to tell you about Meg's pony camp. It's doing really well and a great asset to the community.'

'Oh yeah—sounds like another of her impulsive schemes.'

Mack cringed at the sound of bitterness in his brother-in-law's voice. This was so unlike Joe to be full of resentment. He could sense the deep hurt in the man's heart.

'You need to go look for yourself. The last camp is this weekend as she closes it down for the winter to rest the ponies and the ground. Perhaps you can participate and see how rewarding it is to work with some of the children who have disabilities—she seems to have a way with them. After the weekend, she'll be free if you can spare the time to have some recreation together.'

'Thanks, Mack. It's not as simple as all that now, is it? Especially with this doctor friend of hers hanging around. I'll go find a room for the night at the hotel and sleep on it. I'll phone you in the morning and let you know where I am and what I decide to do.'

As Joe left the house abruptly and drove off, Mack realised he was embarrassed about his situation and pride had risen its ugly head.

Jessie stood next to Mack, taking hold of his hand as if she knew the anguish churning deep inside him.

'We've got to do something,' said Mack. 'We can't sit back and let their marriage go down the drain.'

****

Doctor Joshua Douglas followed Meg out onto the patio with a mug of coffee in his hand. Meg's face brimmed with delight, lapping up his attention. She'd provided him with a light meal and now they relaxed in the sun, soaking up the last days of autumn before the icy southern winter set in.

'That was a good game we had today. I don't suppose we'll get much tennis in during the winter,' said Joshua. 'The grass court is abysmal. I hope the council will build asphalt courts as they have in Queenstown.'

'I wouldn't worry, as the school has a good asphalt basketball court with a net and I heard we can play there. It's only open to local residents.'

'Anyway—I've got something more important on my mind.'

'Oh dear—that sounds ominous.'

'I hope not.' He took her hand as his brown eyes gleamed when his gaze met hers.

Meg began to giggle then stopped. It was obvious Joshua was serious.

'Meg, I've been falling for you in a big way and I'm hoping you'd agree to take our friendship to the next level. I've been waiting for the right moment to ask you ... so I guess it's now. I've only just found the nerve.' He raised his brows, keeping his eyes fixed on her face.

Meg almost dropped her cup. Her mouth fell open as she pulled her hand from his grip.

'I ... sorry, Joshua ... you've taken me completely by surprise. I thought we were just tennis buddies and good friends. I mean ... we haven't really been dating or anything.'

'Oh, no, I hope I haven't scared you off—I've been falling in love with you and I thought I'd made it obvious.'

The phone started ringing just as he pulled her towards him and planted his full lips on hers. She pulled back suddenly.

'Look—this is all happening a bit too fast for me. I'm not even divorced and I don't want to be, either.'

The phone rang again then stopped.

Joshua started biting his lip then wiped his brow.

'I'm so sorry ... I seem to have been reading too much into our friendship. Do I have a chance ... or have you made your mind up?'

The phone continued to ring. Meg stood up. 'Excuse me. I'll have to take that. I'm running my last camp this weekend, and that may be a cancellation. I'll have to get on.'

She bustled into the office but the phone stopped again before she could pick up the receiver.

'Jolly thing. It was probably one of the children cancelling,' she muttered as she hurried back to the patio.

'I'm sorry, Joshua—I have to get ready for pony camp tomorrow and check my bookings. Can I call you tomorrow evening?'

'That's fine. I thought we could have a pleasant, relaxing evening together tonight, but I'll catch up with you then.'

Joshua grabbed his jacket and drove off, putting his foot on the pedal harder than usual, not thinking that children from nearby farms could be riding down the road. Meg stood in the carpark shaking her head as he disappeared onto the highway.

Back in her lounge a short time later, she reached up to draw the curtains when the sound of a vehicle hurtling down the driveway startled her. Had Joshua left something behind? When she took another look she could see it was Walter's truck. What would he be doing calling on her at this time of the day? Her stomach churned as she walked towards the door.

****

After knocking on the door, Walter yanked off his boots and slammed each one against the ornate porch railing to loosen the dirt. Meg held the front door open.

'Sorry, lassie, I'm coming.'

'Why are you removing the mud from your boots when you have to walk back to the carpark in them?'

Walter flashed her a wry smile exposing the fact that he'd recently lost a tooth. He didn't tell her he'd packed an overnight bag and left it in the truck.

'I'll put the kettle on, Grandad. You're staying for dinner, aren't you? There's a steak and kidney pie in the fridge I removed from the freezer yesterday.'

Walter planted himself down in the lounge on one of Meg's wicker, bucket chairs. 'Sure will, thanks. I never turn down an offer like that. You know I'm partial to steak and kidney. It reminds me of your grandmother. She used to bake one for me once a week.'

'Mine is a bit different from the usual pies. I use fresh thyme for extra flavour.'

'I'll give anything a try, my dear. But that's not what I'm here for—although I'm always a starter for home cooking. I'll get down to the brass tacks.'

Meg joined him with the tea and began pouring it.

'Oh—that sounds serious.' Her hand shook as she passed him a mug of tea before she sat down.

'What brings you here, Grandad? Is everything alright with you?'

'Nothing the matter with me, but there's a fair bit of drama going on in your life right now.'

Meg placed her cup back on the table and wrinkled up her nose. 'What do you mean?'

'Did you know that Joe is in town? He has been out to Reed Station in a right state telling Mack and Jessie his troubles. In fact, Mack was going to phone and warn you.'

Walter washed back his tea with noisy gulps and sat back in the chair crossing his legs, glaring at Meg with clasped hands.

'Sorry, Grandad—I don't understand—what's this all about? I haven't heard from Joe—at least not recently. The phone rang a few times earlier but I couldn't get to it in time.'

'He came to Glenorchy to surprise you yesterday, but as he drove through town, he saw you fraternising with that doctor you are friendly with. He was watching you by the lake.'

'I had no idea he would turn up unexpectedly. I wasn't doing anything wrong. Why didn't he approach me instead of spying?'

'He could see you were pretty chummy and jumped to conclusions. I was in the kitchen when he arrived to see Mack and overheard the whole conversation. He offloaded a heap of angst onto Mack as he thought you were having an affair.'

'Oh, poor Joe. Where is he now—is he still at the station?'

'No, he's staying in town somewhere. If you phone Mack, Joe said he would let him know where he is staying.'

'When is he going back to Wellington? He's come such a long way.' Meg stood up and paced the floor, trying to decide a plan of action.

'He flew into Queenstown and has a rental car. After seeing you at the lake, he wanted to return in the morning, but Mack convinced him to stay and give you a chance, although he's reluctant to do so. You'll have to find out where he's staying if you want to chase after him.'

Before Walter finished the sentence, Meg rushed off to her office to phone Mack. She spoke for five minutes then returned to the lounge with arms hanging limp at her sides, her eyes glazed and staring downwards.

'Mack hasn't heard from Joe yet but he expects him to call.'

'Well, we'll just have to have a good chat and wait for Mack to let you know when he hears something. How about some of that homemade pie you promised me.'

'Don't you want to get back home before dark? I'll sit here and wait for Mack's call after we've had our meal.'

Walter gave a lopsided grin. 'I hope you don't mind, lass, but I plan to stay the night if you can give me one of your guest rooms. My kit is in the truck and I think we're in for a long talk later.'

'Oh, really? That's no problem. I'll show you to your room before dinner if you want to grab your kit out of the truck. I'll heat up the pie while you do that.'

Walter trundled back inside with his overnight bag and dumped it in the room Meg had prepared for him. She rolled back the goose-down duvet and plumped up the pillows.

'There's a wall heater on a thermostat and I've turned it on to low. The bathroom is opposite.'

'Don't fuss over me girl. Let's get this meal—I'm looking forward to it. How about some of that apple cider you keep in your fridge?'

After the meal, they retired to the lounge where Meg lit the fire.

'I think we'll need a fire from now on. That southerly wind is freezing at night although it has been lovely and sunny this week.'

Walter leaned forward in his chair pushing the palms of his hands towards the fire for a few minutes then sat back, resting his arms on his knees.

'Do you remember when I told you that I had inherited Reed Station?'

Meg sat down and stretched her legs to warm her feet.

'Yes, I do, although you didn't elaborate and told me that it was a tough life and my grandmother Hazel found it hard. That's all I can remember you telling me.'

Meg sagged as she continued to listen.

'You seem to have this fantasy that the high country life is glamorous and idyllic but you're deceiving yourself. You haven't trudged across ground when it has rained for weeks and every step you take sinks deep into the mud—when it's so cold that your eyebrows freeze over, and worst of all, seeing your prize newborn lambs or calves—sometimes hundreds of them frozen into blocks of ice from heavy snowfalls in spring. Oh yes—and waking in the night to the piercing bellow of a prize bull lying on its back in a creek.'

Walter pulled out a handkerchief to catch a drip at the end of his nose before continuing.

'Reed Station, which was in the Reed Family Trust, was owned by my father's uncle, a bachelor who passed it on to my brother Jack, the eldest son in our family. My own parents had owned a smallholding of land in Dunedin which they used for market gardening and Dad was killed in a tractor accident. Mum died several years later in the flu epidemic.'

'When did you meet Grandma?' Meg asked with a brittle voice.

'Before I took over Reed Station, I worked as a farm labourer in Tekapo, the McKenzie country, and there I met your grandmother while joining a sheep muster on her folks' farm. We fell in love and a year later married in the Church of the Good Shepherd on the edge of Lake Tekapo.'

The light from the flames danced on his face, illuminating deep furrows in his brow as he gazed into the fire.

'Your grandmother and I lived and worked on her parents' farm until they went bankrupt as a result of a major drought. They were able to keep their house and a small block of land which they turned into crops.'

'So how did you come to own Reed Station?' By now, Meg's face appeared animated.

'I inherited it when my Uncle died. It was offered to Jack first and just as your own father had no interest in farming, nor did he and so it was handed to me by default.'

'Time for a cup of tea yet, Grandad?' Meg sat on the edge of her seat as if she was ready to dart off.

'No, wait! There's more and I want you to listen hard, Meg. You may find what I have to say life-changing!'

Meg sat back, her eyes not leaving Walter's face.

He cleared his throat then continued as the firelight exposed his frozen tears.

'The land on Reed Station was rugged, unbroken high country in those days. The roads were almost non-existent and we travelled on the TSS Earnslaw steamship if we wanted to go to Queenstown to pick up supplies—as and when it stopped at the wharf in Glenorchy. Hazel became pregnant with your father after two miscarriages and went to stay with her parents in their humble home in Tekapo. While she remained there to have the baby, I got myself established on the station. Hazel joined me when Len was a few months old, but the remote and harsh lifestyle eventually affected her health. Life in the high country was too tough for her and I can now put it down to my own selfish ambition and short-sightedness that I missed seeing how this was affecting her. Then against Hazel's wishes, when he was only seven I sent your father to boarding school. This embittered him so much that when he finished his schooling he wanted nothing to do with the station or me. We had arguments galore as to why he did not want to take it over which eventually made me lose my cool and throw him out. This broke Hazel's heart as she had already suffered so much—first her babies then Len and later her health. Most of all, your father was the love of her life and she never really forgave me for telling him to leave.'

When Walter finished speaking, he hung his head low and the tone in his voice matched his demeanour—flat and hollow. He sat propped up on his elbows with his head in his hands.

Meg's eyes welled up as she dived into her jacket pocket, fumbled then came out with an embroidered handkerchief to wipe her eyes.

'I'm really sorry to hear all this, Grandad. It's so sad—but you mustn't blame yourself for Grandma's death. You didn't cause her pneumonia.'

Walter lifted his head pulling a large, tartan handkerchief from his jacket pocket. He blew his nose like a foghorn then continued—this time his voice kept breaking up.

'I broke Hazel's heart even though I loved her so much—but I was hard and selfish and all I could think about was building a successful station.'

'Oh, please don't upset yourself, Grandad. That's all in the past and your relationship with Dad and the family is mended now.'

Walter looked Meg in the eye.

'Don't you know why I'm telling you this, my girl? I can see you going down the same track with Joe. From what I hear, he has been suffering as a result of your grandiose plans.'

Meg's face dropped. Her nose began to twitch and she sat back in her chair, wrenching her hands and rolling her wedding ring.

'What do you mean by suffering? He'd agreed to come to Glenorchy—I thought he liked the idea of being in the country.'

Walter frowned and set his jaw.

'You couldn't see past your own nose, to be honest, Meg. You were so focused on your own ambitions that you hadn't considered where Joe would fit into your devices and plans. He thinks you have lost interest in him and that he doesn't count anymore, just as I had made Hazel feel. Don't make the same mistake as I did or you'll live to regret it.'

Meg's face paled. She hesitated before saying anything.

'Oh, Grandad—I didn't know I'd hurt Joe. I just thought he would rather be back in the city working as a corporate businessman than live here with me.'

'No, Meg. You drove him away and could have made him sick. If you want to avoid a life of deep regret, you need to go after him and make amends any way you can before it's too late.'

Meg stood up and walked over to the frail-looking man who had come to save her marriage. She threw herself at him, wrapping her arms around his neck.

He took her hand. 'Luckily for you, your father is the person Hazel and I made—despite my treatment of him he rose to the occasion and became a success for himself—but the guilt I've been carrying has coloured my life all this time. It's only since Mack eased himself into it that things have changed for the better, and now I have to pinch myself on occasions to believe just how wonderful my life has become.'

'I'll go and see Joe, honest Grandad and I'll try to put things right with him. Please pray that he'll forgive me.'

'It's time to sort your own life out. I've been praying for you both all this time, just as I do for the rest of the family. Now it's your turn to do something.'

'I promise you things will be different—if only I can track him down tomorrow.'

'Mack is going to phone you early in the morning after Joe has called him to say where he is staying.'

Meg rubbed her lined eyes while her translucent, porcelain cheeks screamed out for sleep.

'Hope you don't mind—I'd like to have an early night. Will you be okay? Spare blankets are in the wardrobe. I'll make you breakfast before you leave.'

'I'll be fine and don't worry about breakfast. I'll have it back at the station.'

'Thanks again, Grandad. Night-night.' She bent over and kissed his cheek, leaving him to ponder the glowing embers of a dying fire.

****

The rooster crowed earlier than usual, long before the rest of the household had risen. Bessie got up early and off out the door. It was her weekend off and this time her friends in Arrowtown had invited her to stay.

Jessie was already busy feeding the babies who'd wakened early. Mack stumbled out of bed, wandering into the nursery tripping over toys underfoot that they'd forgotten to pick up the night before.

'You're already up feeding?' Mack took Oliver from her and placed him over his shoulder. She took Will from his cot and started feeding him.

'That jolly rooster started up early making a terrible racket. He hasn't done that for ages. Didn't you hear him?'

'No—I only heard the shower when Bessie got ready to go out.' Jessie propped Will over her knee and patted his back gently.

'She's off to Arrowtown to stay with her friend and won't be back until Sunday evening.'

Jessie looked at Mack with a compassionate gaze. 'How are you feeling this morning after such a hard time with Joe? What do you think will happen?'

'I'm feeling a bit rough. We need to wait a bit as he said he would phone and let me know what he decides this morning.'

'Perhaps you'd best get dressed, love. You may need to pay Meg a visit if Joe takes off back to Wellington and gives up on her. She'll probably spit out her dummy when she finds out.'

'Let's not think the worst. Wait for him to call.'

Mack sat at the breakfast table a short time later poking at his scrambled eggs with his fork and leaning the side of his head on one hand.

Jessie had concern for her husband who was so generous-hearted towards others. 'Coffee? It's freshly made.'

Mack lifted his head and forced a smile. 'Thanks. It's a pity all this is happening when Grandad seems to be so happy these days enjoying the twins and life in general after a difficult life.'

He reached for the strawberry jam and scooped a large dollop with a spoon dropping it on his toast. He had no sooner finished speaking when the phone rang.

'I'll get it,' said Jessie, licking her fingers and wiping them on the sides of her trousers. She hurried to pick up the phone and returned waving at Mack to come.

'Quick, it's Joe. He just asked for you and he sounds distressed.'

'Okay, tell him I'll be there.'

Mack raced into the office and picked up the phone. He kept quiet and just kept nodding his head while Jessie stood watching. From what she heard, Joe seemed to be offloading a lot more on poor Mack who finally spoke up. 'I think you're making a huge mistake if you leave now without seeing Meg and what she has achieved at Willow Park. As I said last night—I know she loves you and doesn't want to lose you.'

'Well, she didn't give me much indication of that before I left. I'm feeling too disappointed with her.'

'I think you need to search your own heart and find it in you to forgive her and then pay her a visit.'

Mack clenched his teeth and shook his head while Jessie stood in the doorway waiting for the verdict. A few minutes silence on Joe's part then he hung up.

'It's no good, Jessie—he says he's going back to Wellington today.'

'Where is he staying—has he checked out yet? Maybe it's not too late to go and talk to him again.'

'He's staying at the Glenorchy Hotel. Says he's checking out at twelve. I'm sure he's still trying to decide what to do as he probably doesn't want to lose Meg. I'm going to phone and encourage her to go to the hotel and convince Joe to stay. The ball is in her court now.'

While Mack went back to the office to ring Meg, Jessie sat in the lounge slumped in a chair, quietly praying. She heard a vehicle door closing and Bluey making the kind of racket he usually did when one of the family arrived home. It was Walter, just in time for breakfast.

Mack came off the phone passing Jessie in the kitchen as she cracked fresh eggs into the frying pan while Walter walked through the door looking the worse for wear.

'Great, Grandad—just in time for a good breakfast and then we can catch up about Meg after that. We're waiting for Joe to phone and tell me what he decides.'

'Thanks, Mack. It has certainly been a mammoth task talking sense into her, but I'm convinced she's going to ditch her doctor friend and reconcile with Joe. Let's talk after I've had time to eat and clean up. Morning Prayer first.'

Chapter Eighteen

Meg hurried into the room where her grandfather spent the night, and stripped the bed. Today there was an older group arriving mid-morning and because of her predicament, Sara, her horse coach would have to manage along with the team leader.

She stood in front of the mirror tiding her hair and opened her makeup bag. Since she'd lived at Willow Park and had become involved with the horses, she hadn't bothered much with her appearance unless she accompanied Joshua on an outing. Even then, it wasn't for him but just to make her feel as though she wasn't a complete frump. The red lipstick she applied to her lips lifted her sallow complexion as she gazed into the mirror. 'That looks better,' she muttered.

A light tap on the door brought her back to reality.

Her coach stood at the front door. 'Are you there, Meg?'

'When should we bring the horses down for the first session?'

'Oh, hi, Sara—I won't be starting schooling until one o'clock. Before lunch I want you and the volunteers to take the children through grooming and tacking. A few of the horses appeared to have muddy coats when I saw them yesterday. They may need washing with warm water. Use a bucket, not the hose. It's too cold at this time of year—but you know all that, sorry, Sara—I'm trying to tell Grandma how to suck eggs.' They both burst into laughter.

'I'm sorry—I have to run an urgent errand in town. I'll see you back here by one and if not, you know the drill—you're in charge.'

Meg picked up her handbag, took one more look at herself in the mirror, straightened the collar of her shirt-blouse and shot out the door. As she stepped into her car, the heel of her shoe slid on something squishy. It was horse poo. *This is the last straw—what more could go wrong today?* She crumpled forward on the steering wheel and let out a loud wail. At last, she could release her pent-up tension from the previous twenty-four hours, but in case one of the staff could see her, she held back her sobs and started the engine. Once she was on the main road, she pulled over and cleaned her shoe with an old rag. Pulling the rear vision mirror closer, she examined her wet cheeks, dabbing them with the handkerchief she had pulled from her handbag.

While driving to the Glenorchy Hotel, she rehearsed all that she would say to Joe. Will he be receptive or would he tell her to stay away and leave him alone?

The carpark at the hotel was almost full. Not far from the vehicles was the hotel Reception with a small cobblestone courtyard out front.

As Meg walked through the entranceway, she spotted cigarette butts strewn along the sides of the footpath. She crossed the courtyard, entering the main door of the reception area and gagged. The stale stench of beer and cigarette smoke made her retch.

'Sorry about that mess outside. I could see you screwing up your face at the filthy butts. The smell comes inside here too. I'll have to find someone to go out and sweep up, as I'm too busy here at Reception. They are the tourists who have the campervans down by the lake. They come here and drink then sit outside and smoke. They never adhere to the signage that tells them to smoke out back in the designated area. How can I help you? Sorry—we have no vacancies and Saturday is our busiest day so you need to book in advance. We're the only hotel between here and Queenstown.'

The buxom woman with inappropriate attire didn't give Meg a chance to speak and had made assumptions.

'I'm not looking for a room—I'm meeting one of your guests here.'

The woman moved her spectacles from where they perched on top of her head to her eyes. 'Oh, silly me—I should have asked first. What's your guest's name?'

'Joe Wilds is his name. He stayed last night.'

'Ah yes ... Mr Wilds has made an arrangement to check out late... midday in fact.'

'That's right. Is he in his room?'

The woman phoned and spoke to Joe. She placed the receiver back on the hook and pointed along the corridor.

'Room nine, next to the lift.'

Meg trudged along the length of the corridor. The old-fashioned paisley wallpaper caught her attention as she glanced at the room numbers, but Room Nine was not near Reception as expected. The numbers went from the opposite direction and Joe's room was towards the end of the long corridor.

As she reached the door, she stood transfixed, gaping at the doorknob. She'd already forgotten how she would greet him when he opened the door. The butterflies in her stomach caused her muscles to tighten as her knuckles of one hand tapped three times on the door. She held her breath.

The door swung open causing her to stumble backwards, losing her balance in her high-heeled shoes. A crimson flush swam up her neck to her face.

'Oh—hi Joe! Do you mind if I come in?'

'I suppose you can—you're here now,' he snapped.

The door went to close automatically before Joe held it back for her. 'Have a seat over there. They aren't that comfortable, but it's all I have.'

Meg gave him a sideways glance as she brushed past him. His face appeared drawn with dark rings around his dachshund eyes. She plopped herself into the chair and directed her gaze out the window towards the sky.

'Would you like anything to drink? There's not much here except packets of tea and coffee. Nothing cold, sorry.'

As Meg turned her eyes met his. 'Tea will be fine, thanks.'

Joe stood at the tiny alcove in the bedroom suite and turned the kettle on. 'So—what brings you here all of a sudden? I'm checking out today. Did Mack ask you to come? You know he rang me?'

'I came of my own volition but he did tell me you were leaving today. He said you saw me at the lake with my friend Joseph and jumped to conclusions.'

Joe bristled. Meg could see his face in the wardrobe mirror. It had turned tomato red. He cleared his throat. Meg startled as he slammed the metal teapot on the tray before he filled it.

'Yes, I did see you with your fancy man. I'm not hanging around here to play second fiddle to anyone. I'm leaving in a few hours.'

He carried the tray to the desk near Meg and poured her tea, trying to remain as civil as possible.

Meg stood up. 'Please, Joe. Hear me out. You've got it all wrong. I haven't been unfaithful to you at all.'

Joe left his cup of tea sitting on the tray next to Meg's and sat on the bed, as there was only one chair in the room. Meg walked over and sat next to him. She turned to him and took his hand which he pulled away.

'Joe, I love you. You are the one who walked away and went back to Wellington—all because I'd been overzealous with my business plans. I've been so lonely and have been waiting for you to return.'

'So what's with this doctor fella? You seemed pretty chummy when I saw you.'

'He's a lonely widower and has offered me companionship, nothing else ... that is ... until yesterday.'

'What do you mean? What have you done?' He glared at her, keeping his eyes fixed on her face.

'Quite unexpectedly, he asked for a commitment—says he loves me. I made it clear I'm a married woman and do not want a divorce. We haven't even dated yet and I'm not in love with him,

Joe. He's got the wrong idea, honest he has.' Meg's voice quivered. She tried to hold back the tears that formed pools in her eyes as she scratched around in her bag for her handkerchief but Joe thrust his own one into her hand.

'It's clean—carry on—I'm all ears,' he said, his own voice beginning to crackle.

'I've never wanted anyone else but you. Please come home and see what I've been doing with the pony camp. It's a proper business—one that the whole town admires. It has helped a lot of families. Just come and give it a chance … give me a chance.'

Joe picked up his cup and gulped down the last of his tea while Meg let her cup go cold. He took a long look at her face.

'Come here.' He wrapped his octopus arms around her, squeezing her tight.

Meg kissed him tenderly. 'You know … it's all I've been hoping for … that you would do this. I'm so sorry for the pain I've caused you, Joe. I just wanted to be successful, just as you and Dad were with the export company. Even Grandad and Mack are running a thriving sheep and beef station. I wanted something for myself to feel I'd achieved something worthwhile in life.'

'I'm sorry too, for being so judgemental. I never meant to hurt you but your property development scheme would have been a complete disaster.'

Meg took his hand. 'Can we start again, from scratch?'

Joe looked her in the eye. 'I guess it's time we started doing some work on our marriage.'

'Let's get back home. I need you to help with the children today. Would you mind?'

'I suppose that's okay—I'll give it a go, although my skills are more in the business line. My suitcase is packed and I'll book out at Reception now.'

Joe had a last look around the room in case he'd forgotten something and shut the door with Meg in tow following along the passageway.

'So, I'm going to be a horsey person now, am I? Just like the old days in Wellington when I helped you with your horses in the stables. Good thing I've got experience, eh?' He winked as Meg helped him carry some of his luggage out to Reception.

'I must phone Mack when we get in. They'll be wanting to celebrate and so will Grandad. Thank you for not giving up on me.'

'We have some work to do on our relationship yet. I'll see you at home.' He stepped into the vehicle and wound the window down.

'Right, madam—here we come, Willow Park.' He winked at her as he started the engine.

Meg leaned through the window and kissed his cheek. 'See you back there soon.'

'Looks like I'm going to be your new volunteer assistant at pony camp,' He revved up the engine before careering off down the road. Meg climbed into her car and took off in close pursuit.

Within minutes she arrived at Willow Park to see Joe standing next to his vehicle with his suitcase and extra luggage propped up against the car. A wide grin stretched across her face until she remembered there was a certain person she would have to phone, right away. Her smile faded quickly forcing the corners of her mouth downwards like a sad clown.

'If you're happy to have me back home, tell your face that,' remarked Joe, in a teasing tone.

'It's not you, Joe. I'm ecstatic you're home. I have some unfinished business to deal with and it's making my stomach churn.'

'You mean about telling your doctor friend your change in circumstances. That shouldn't be too hard—just tell him the truth.'

'I'll give him a call later.'

They both carried Joe's luggage up the path to the house.

The staff had the horses lined up in their outside stalls ready for the one o'clock riding session. Sara and her assistant stood encircled by the group of riders.

Meg went inside the house with Joe to offload his luggage when he pulled her aside.

'Leave my luggage—just dump it in the bedroom. I think we need to have a good talk before you go out there. We have a few things to straighten out first.'

Meg stood still. She appeared taken aback by his directness.

'Of course, love. Let's sit down in the living room and close the door. Sara knows the drill and doesn't need me out there all the time.' Joe followed her into the lounge which was out of bounds to the guests and sat opposite Meg. He asserted himself before she had the chance to jump in first.

'I came back because I love you—but I need you to know how much you hurt me by your self-centred behaviour. You didn't once consider my needs or respect me when I opposed your grand plans and designs nor did you allow me to have an opinion about our joint ventures—in fact, it seemed they were only your projects. I didn't figure in your plans and I don't want that to happen again.'

Meg's face turned pink. She took off her jacket and rubbed the back of her neck. Before she could open her mouth to reply, Joe jumped in, no holds barred.

'All the time you were plotting and planning, I tried to have some input, but you shut me down every time making me feel useless—disempowered. That's why I took off. I thought I had no value in your life, but I never stopped loving you. I started praying that you would have a change of heart.'

Meg's eyes glazed over. She stared at the ground, shell-shocked.

Joe continued. 'Then when I saw you fraternising with your doctor friend, it finished me—I couldn't take any more. Before you came to see me at the hotel, I thought our marriage was at an end and was ready to pack it in and head back to Wellington for good.'

Meg lifted her head and looked at him. Her eyes swam with tears as she stood up and approached him, her voice croaking as she answered.

'Please forgive me, Joe. I had no idea of the effect all this had on you and how insensitive I've been. Frankly, the way you describe it makes me sound like a selfish prat—but I'm not the same person now. God has removed my obsession to be famous or successful. I just want to help others and make a difference in people's lives.'

Joe reached out his hand and drew her close to him.

'Come and sit with me—please. I'm not trying to shame you, Meg. It's just vital that you know how it impacted me and that I can't live like that anymore—but I believe you and I can see it's unlikely you'll put me through that again. So here I am—boring stuffed shirt and all.' He enveloped her tightly.

'I hope you can bring yourself to forgive me properly, one day. I know you'll be testing the waters, Joe. But we both want this marriage to work. Let's start over again.' She kissed him on the cheek. 'We can work at it, one day at a time.'

'Don't you have a field full of children waiting for you to show up with this man of yours?'

'Oh, don't worry. I told the staff you've been working on a contract in Wellington. Now I can tell them your contract there is finished and you'll now be part of the business—I mean our business. This is our pony camp.'

'You'd best go and get changed. The afternoon session will be over before you get started. I'll wait outside.'

Joe wandered out to the patio and sat down in the sun stretching his legs as he scanned his estate. The furrows in his brow had gone and the muscles in his jaw softened.

Within a short time, Meg appeared in beige Jodhpurs and black jacket, looking professional.

'Mmm, you look quite the part. Come on, I'll be right behind you.'

Meg wandered over to speak to Sara, her coach.

'Hi Sara, this is my husband, Joe. He'll be running pony camp with me in future.'

Joe shook Sara's hand. 'We're glad of the help today. I hear you're good with horses but don't ride— is that right?'

'Yes, I'd rather keep my feet on the ground, but I don't mind handling them. I've had plenty of experience doing that with Meg's horses in Wellington at the stables.'

'Excuse me interrupting, Sara—how are you going—are they all here?' Meg picked up Sara's clipboard with the list of children that had registered and glanced down the list.

'No, Bonny was on the list but her mother rang to cancel as she has a cold. You'll probably get a call from her tonight. Apparently, Mack invited her to spend a day on their station and she hopes to bring her out one weekend.'

'That's right. I'll pass the message on to Mack—we'd better get started. Are the cavaletti poles set up in the arena? I want the new riders to work on those first.'

Sara looked around to see the volunteers returning from setting up the course. 'Yes, they've just finished.'

Meg approached the staff. 'Now some of you haven't met my husband, Joe. He'll be with us for the rest of this camp, now that his contract has finished in Wellington.'

Sara flashed a glance at her sidekick, Petra, her team leader who covered her mouth to hide a grin.

Meg's neck flushed. She'd always been a private person but the fact that she'd been on her own for several months meant that Joe's sudden homecoming created a trickle of sensation amongst the staff.

Joe lifted his Stetson and bowed his head. Sara stepped in and gave the staff new instructions while Joe looked relieved as they followed the coach back into the arena.

At this final camp, there were no children with special needs so the guestrooms were empty and Joe and Meg had the whole lodge to themselves. Occasionally a few of the younger children were afraid to sleep in the outside bunkrooms and requested to sleep inside. This weekend the camp consisted of older children who all slept in the outside accommodation in the custom-built arena bunkhouse. A few of them still enjoyed dossing down directly on the hay bales in sleeping bags.

Meg tugged on Joe's sleeve. 'Would you like to watch our first afternoon session once it's underway? Later you might like to help me put the covers on the horses for the night. We let them graze in the paddock closest to the stables and catch them again in the morning. It's too much to expect the volunteers to do it all so I always give them a hand.'

Meg's agenda was by no means hidden. She was intent on getting Joe involved with her new venture as fast as possible. That, she considered, was a sure way of ensuring he was there to stay.

Although she still commandeered, it was in a good way. Organising people was her greatest strength—that her husband well knew.

Joe draped his torso over a fence rail watching the group preparing for the afternoon session. Meg scurried down the path and stood next to him.

'Show me the way,' said Joe. 'I can remember some of the things I did to help you in Wellington when you had your horses in the stables. I might need to brush up on a few things—I'm sure you'll put me right.' He chuckled as they wandered down to the outside arena.

'Ah—yuk!' Joe's boot skidded in a pile of horse dung. 'That part of it I forgot about.'

Meg grinned warmly as he scraped his boot along the grass to clean it. Her eyes searched along the fence line. 'There's a poo bucket around here somewhere. The volunteers usually go along and scoop it up. Ah—there it is—I'll just clear it away while you join the group by the arena. If you wait over there by the gate, I'll meet up with you in a minute.'

Joe walked over and picked up the scoop. 'Please let me.'

He happily scooped up the dung and dumped it in the bucket with a small shovel while Meg looked on in her element. It looked like Joe was there to stay, and judging by his cheerful demeanour, he approved of her enterprise. As soon as they arrived at the arena, he set about helping one of the riders tighten her horse's girth.

Sara raced up to him. 'Hi, there, Joe. Meg has told me so much about you. It must have been a nuisance having to travel backwards and forwards to Wellington for your work.'

Meg arrived just in time to rescue Joe from Sara who'd put him on the spot and spun an elaborate story about Joe having to work away from home. It was the truth, but not the whole truth, and it wouldn't do any harm keeping that part quiet, Meg convinced herself.

Before Joe answered, Meg intervened. 'Joe, would you mind helping me set up the cross-rails for the jumping exercise? Sara is busy organising the riders.'

'Sure, no problem.' He willingly followed her to the other side of the arena. 'I'll bet you weren't prepared for us to throw you in the deep end,' said Meg with a wry smile.

They set up two low jumps with cross-rails.

'This is for the more experienced riders,' said Meg. 'We don't do anything too advanced. They can do that at their pony clubs. It's mainly to give them a bit of the country life for those who live in town and during the week I let local riders use the arena. They often set up a few jumps themselves.'

When they had finished, Joe took hold of Meg's arm.

'Are you going to be busy for the rest of the day? I hoped we could get some time together to talk about where we go from here.'

Meg took his hand and clasped it. His eyes met hers.

'I want that too, Joe. I'm sorry, but I have to supervise for the rest of the afternoon. The coach manages the children but I'm ultimately responsible for health and safety and need to be here—especially when they are jumping. The rest are just unqualified volunteers apart from the paid staff members, Sara and Petra.'

Joe looked awkward. 'Oh, I see—of course, you do.'

'Let's go over to the arena.'

When they arrived, Sara had begun giving her staff instructions as the program commenced, while Meg and Joe chatted at the sideline.

Meg said quietly, 'Let's go up and sit on the patio. We can watch them from there. They are in Sara's capable hands for now. As long as the crew know where I am. I'll just let her know.'

After talking to Sara, Meg hurried up to the house and brought out a jug of fresh lemonade and two glasses and placed them on the patio table.

'Good thing the arena is close by—I can see everything from here and they know where I am.'

'Thanks, Meg. I appreciate you giving up your time today—especially when you had no idea I would make a surprise appearance.'

He lounged back in the garden chair, stretching his arms out at his sides yawning, enjoying the sun.

Meg tousled his hair as she passed him. 'This is freshly squeezed lemonade with mint.'

They sat drinking their iced beverages watching the riders tackle their program. Joe's face adopted a serious look. Although the shadows around his eyes had lessened, the deep furrows in his brow were evident still.

'Meg—before I return to Wellington on Monday, I need to be certain you are fully committed to our marriage and won't change your mind again. I couldn't go through it again.'

Meg sat aghast. Her nose twitched the way it always did when she was nervous. She stood up and pulled her chair closer to him then held his hand, her stare penetrating his eyes.

'Oh, dear Joe. You have got me so wrong—to think that I would deliberately hurt or deceive you. Honestly—when you left for Wellington the first time, I was so worried you would never return. Since then I've discovered that it was my selfish ambition and self-centeredness that drove you away.'

Joe didn't stir or refute her confession while he took it all in.

'I wanted to turn my life around and prove to you that I could change but didn't know how. Mack came up with this idea of running a pony camp and use my qualifications working with children—even those with disabilities who benefit from equine therapy too.'

Joe found his tongue. 'That's good. I knew deep down that you had it in you to make a difference and I just couldn't understand why you seemed to sabotage everything we had set before us to live a good life. Now I can see that you have changed so maybe it's time I resigned from the company and put the house back on the market.'

The two sat observing the horses trotting around the arena, listening to Sara call out her commands while the late autumn sun poured onto the patio saturating them with warmth.

Meg peered at him pleadingly with eyes like midnight jasper. 'Would you mind helping tomorrow? We are short of a side walker to accompany the new riders, as we are one volunteer down. It'll keep you fit, running next to a trotting horse and we need to keep the children safe.'

'With pleasure—I won't feel so redundant. At last, we can do something together that unites us.'

A wide smile stretched across Joe's face. He was there to stay.

Chapter Nineteen

Meg lay in Joe's arms, stretched out long on their four-seater leather couch after a light meal of beef stew that the camp cook had prepared. It was Sunday evening. All the children had left Willow Park by four o'clock.

'I'm tired out,' said Meg. 'It's healthy fatigue though, with all that fresh air and exercise running next to trotting horses on a lead. We only do that if they are novices or disabled, to encourage them to trot.'

'I'm tired out too. You're fortunate to have an experienced coach such as Sara. I'm impressed with the setup you have here, Meg. It's all so professional—you've done well.'

'Thanks honey. Would you mind putting a few more logs on that fire while I make that dreaded phone call to you know who?'

'Oh, yes, your friend, Doctor Douglas. That's most important.' Joe winked. 'Don't worry. He's a big boy and can take it.' He lay back staring at the fire then remembered Meg had asked him to put some more logs on while she made the phone call.

A short time later, she walked back into a room that was glowing. They had turned out the lights except for an old lamp and Joe was mesmerised by the flames leaping at the glass door of the Kent fire. His previous animated countenance had left him.

Meg stood in front of the fire warming herself. 'Are you okay—you appear to be miles away? It's freezing in the kitchen tonight. Good thing this camp was the last one before winter arrives.'

Joe redirected his stare from gaping at the fire to Meg.

'How did it go—I'll bet he didn't let you off lightly?'

Meg stammered. 'Oh—he was more understanding than I thought. He said he had unrealistic expectations of me and shouldn't have asked for a commitment so soon, as I wasn't divorced. I told him I was at fault for encouraging him—even though, by that, I meant playing tennis and going on picnics. I said how it must have been a temptation for a lonely man and I apologised to him. Ultimately, we were both walking on thin ice. He seemed indifferent as if he didn't really care. Perhaps he was guarding his heart. Anyway, he said he is ready to move on.'

'So am I,' mumbled Joe. He pulled her close to him. 'I can see how you've changed, Meg. You've become humble—not like the puffed-up woman I knew before I took off to Wellington. Tell me ... what made you change your mind ... was it, Mack?'

'It was initially, but we also have Grandad to thank for showing me the way. He paid me a visit to rescue our marriage.'

'Is that right—what did he say?'

'He came here the night you offloaded our problems onto Mack and Jessie. He'd heard your distress from the kitchen and took off out the back door and drove over here to see me. I put him up in one of the guest rooms and we stayed up half the night talking. He told me a story about the way he had neglected Grandma Hazel and how his selfish ambition and self-centeredness had sabotaged his own marriage. He even attributes her ill health and subsequent death to their harsh lifestyle living on Reed Station in the early days, before the land had been broken.'

'Oh, really? Poor Walter beating himself up like that. He shouldn't blame himself—I'm sure he couldn't have been that bad.'

'He was just so intent on building his farming empire that he neglected to see how hard it was for a young woman with a toddler. Life was too harsh for Grandma in those days. She suffered, but I don't believe he was to blame for her death. He has just perceived it that way.'

'What are you trying to tell me, Meg? Was Walter trying to draw a parallel to our lives?'

'He meant that I probably neglected to see the stress that I'd put you under while chasing my own dreams—pipedreams they were.'

Joe enveloped her with his arms.

'I think you and I should think about renewing our marriage vows when I get back from Wellington. How about it?'

Meg sat bolt upright, holding both his hands.

'Really, Joe? I'd love that. How long do you think you'll be in Wellington sorting things out?'

'I'm not sure. But if you don't have any pony camps until after winter, perhaps you can get on a plane and spend some time with me in our house while it is on the market. We won't have to be there the whole time until it sells—just long enough for me to wind up my partnership in the company and sell my shares to the partners.'

'Sure. I'd like that. I'll have to ask Mack if he can take care of the horses while I'm away—or perhaps I can pay Sara and a few of the local volunteers to do that. Charlie will keep an eye on the place but he doesn't know much about caring for the horses.'

'Why don't you ask your folks if they'll come down from Nelson for a while? They may enjoy the break.'

'That's a possibility. They have already spoken about coming down before winter sets in. I'll call them after you go back.'

'A perfect plan. I'm looking forward to our new life together, Meg. Thanks to Walter and Mack.'

'That's for certain. They are two shepherds caring for their flock. We, the family are their flock.'

'Precisely—so why don't we call them the good shepherds—just like the name of that church in Tekapo, *The Church of the Good Shepherd*?'

'Yeah, I like that. The good shepherds—that's exactly what they are.'

****

Mack opened the letter that Bessie handed to him postmarked Wellington.

'Thanks, Bessie—I think it's from Meg and Joe. I'm dying to hear how they're getting on. They've only been away for a fortnight though.'

'Oh, let me know too.'

'I'd better read it out to Jessie first. Where is she?'

'With the farrier in the stables. The twins are with Pru and Wyatt.'

'I can't linger here sorry—I've got to get back to the stockmen and work out a feed budget for the Angus cattle and the horses. Winter will soon be upon us. Have you seen Grandad anywhere—there has been no sign of him all morning?'

'Sorry, Mack. I forgot to tell you he's unwell today. Says he's been getting a few headaches. Maybe he needs to see the doctor.'

Mack's heart sank. Bessie would only mention the doctor if his grandfather was sickening for something. She always knew.

'Is he in bed?'

'Not sure if he's in bed, but he is in his room lying down.'

'I'll get this feed budget sorted out first. The supplier is coming to Glenorchy tomorrow and I can't afford to miss out and need to phone the order through pronto. I'll talk to Grandad tonight and see if we can get him to the doctor this week.'

Mack climbed onto the quad bike and disappeared up the back of the station to find the stockmen who were in one of the feed sheds.

An hour later, Mack met Jessie leading Chantilly back into her paddock. He drove up to the fence slowly to avoid frightening her horse.

'How did you get on with the farrier?'

'He thought she had laminitis in her left hoof but I diagnosed a bad stone bruise which he later concurred. He thinks she needs shoes when I'm riding up and down the stony track. It's different if we only ride the horses on grass or soft ground. What do you think?'

'It's a good idea. You ride her up and down the track often just as I do with Zoro. That's why I've always made sure he has shoes.'

'My horse in Bethlehem didn't need them. I only rode Rusty in the paddocks and if I rode him down to the beach, we walked along the edge of the estuary away from the road. Anyway, the farrier said he'll wait until the swelling has gone down and come back to shoe her.'

Mack started to fidget. 'Look, Jess, I need to tell you about Grandad.'

'Why, what's happened?'

'Nothing yet, but I'm concerned he has started getting the headaches he used to get prior to having a stroke. Bessie said he has taken to his room for the day. We must get him to see the doctor before anything happens.'

'I hope not, poor Grandad—just when he is looking forward to seeing the twins grow up.'

'I know—but he is in his eighties and has already had two strokes. He's living on borrowed time.'

'Mack! Grandad is a tough rooster and will last many years yet. He wants to see his grandsons mustering sheep. He has great plans for them.'

****

Walter was the last patient for the day. He walked back out to the waiting room where Mack who sat patiently, ready to hear the outcome.

'Well—what's the verdict? How many lives have you got left now?' Mack stopped short, catching himself making light of it when it could be serious.

'I'm fine. No stroke looming, he reckons. Blood pressure was on the high side but he said it is to be expected after all the upset with Meg. I didn't expect him to bring that up—in fact, by the look on his face when he saw me walk in, he expected me to give him a rollicking. He only said to take it easy for the rest of the week. I told him that Meg and Joe had reconciled and she is in Wellington with him. He said he knew, and he just wanted her to be happy. I don't hold it against him.'

'Well let's get you home so you can rest. Those grandsons of yours need you to hang around for a lot longer yet.'

On the way back to the station, Mack stopped by Willow Park to check the horses in the paddocks. Just as Meg had instructed the camp staff before she left, the horses had their blankets on and their feed bags contained fresh hay. The staff had put them to bed for the night in the stables. Sara had organised some of the volunteers to tend and exercise them while Meg stayed in Wellington.

Walter waited patiently in the Ute for Mack. 'Come on, Grandad—let's get you home. Everything is shipshape. Meg has it all under control as usual.'

****

Jessie was back working her business part-time, driving her mobile clinic to Kinloch twice a week and one day a week in Glenorchy. She'd employed an on-call vet experienced in anaesthetics to assist her with surgery part-time. Life was hectic, coming home to boisterous twin boys after a tiring workday.

After her last client in Kinloch, she trudged to her bus, plodded up the steps and dumped her medical bag on the bench. She placed her hands on her hips, stretching from side to side, and yawned. Today had been one of the busiest in a while—mostly complicated late births of Angora goats and sheep— just before winter arrived. Now to drive home and put her feet up for a well-deserved rest. Her mother was a Godsend. She couldn't have managed without her with a veterinary business to run and the station to oversee together with her husband.

Mack had already arrived home and sat in front of the fire bouncing Oliver on his knee while Walter lay slumped in his armchair making a sound like the TSS Earnslaw steamship in his sleep.

'Hi, honey.' He screwed up his nose. 'Just in time to change this one.' He grinned at her until he noticed she didn't appreciate his teasing.

'Just joking—looks like you've had another hectic day. I'm just on my way to change him. Your mother has fed them and given them both their bottles.' Mack ambled off down to the nursery while Jessie pushed her feet into her slippers and stood with her back to the fire. Not long after, she joined Mack. They bathed the twins and put them to bed.

'Dinners on the table,' Bessie said as they walked passed the kitchen. 'I ate at midday and I'm off to my room now. The meal is all set up on the table in the crockpot. I'll see you in the morning before I leave for the weekend.'

'Oh, that's right. We've got that young girl Bonny coming to ride Zoro. She's arriving in the morning and going home in the afternoon. I hope she'll fit in all right. Her parents are dropping her off and they are staying at Willow Park for the night. Sara will be staying there too until Meg and Joe get back. It's only for one night so I'm sure Bonny will be okay with us.'

Bessie took herself off to her room. Walter woke just as Mack and Jessie arrived at the dinner table and shuffled in to join them.

'The old joints are stiff. It just came on when we had that drama with Joe but it's starting to settle down, now it's all sorted.'

'We have a guest to entertain this weekend, Grandad. It's that young girl who appears to have the potential to be a horse whisperer. Bonny—Meg's protégé.'

'Is that right?' Walter reached over and helped himself to a large serving of the pie. 'You'll have your work cut out, both of you.'

Mack smiled and darted a glance at Jessie.

'Grandad. We thought you might like to show her your shepherding skills with your dogs before we finish the autumn muster. She hasn't seen it before. I'll get her working with Zoro too. I'm going to let her ride him.'

Jessie passed the tomato sauce around the table.

'Is she ready to ride on the station?'

'She'll only be in the paddock by the woolshed. The shepherds are bringing the sheep down to the bottom grazing areas so they'll be safe during the snowstorms and the ewes will be fattened before lambing. Bonny's mother says the girl wants to be a shepherdess, but I think she's a touch young to decide her future. Anyway, it will be a valuable experience no matter what she does later in life.'

'Shhh ... I think one of the boys has woken up. I'll go and check.'

Chapter Twenty

'Hi, Mack! Where's Zoro?'

The bubbly girl ran towards him while he waited outside the barn. She was just as he had remembered—spirited and full of gusto as she started pulling on the sleeve of his Swaandri jacket.

Mack's eyes shot a warm glance at her mother.

'Wow, Bonny! You're rearing to go, just like Zoro. First, I'd like you to come inside to meet my wee family. Perhaps your Mum would like a cup of tea?'

'Thanks, Mack.' The woman put out her hand. 'I'm Eve. It's good to meet you since Bonny hasn't stopped talking about you and Zoro. I hear you have twin boys now.'

'Yes, we have. You're just in time before they go down for their nap. They've been up since first light. Come with me, Bonny—I'll show you your room.'

After Bonny dropped her bag in the guest room, Jessie put the kettle on for tea and introduced herself and the twins to Bonny and her mother.

The eager girl made sure they kept the time drinking tea and fussing over the baby boys to a minimum. Her constant push to get back to the barn and saddle Zoro won through. No sooner had they finished their morning tea than Pru arrived at the homestead to babysit the twins. Eve greeted Pru then sped off out the driveway back to Willow Park where Bonny's father had a day off, reading and relaxing.

'Thanks, Mum. I appreciate your help today. Now I can spend time with Bonny and Mack as I think I'm in for a unique experience. Would you mind putting the twins to bed for their nap? I'll grab our lunch boxes I packed last night and the water bottles. It could be a long day.'

'I'll get some meat out and prepare the meal. You said Bessie won't be back until late so I can help out before I head home later.'

She wrapped her arms around Pru and kissed her cheek.

'You're a gem. Bessie left a Shepherd's Pie in the fridge. We just need a few vegetables to put with it.'

'I'd better chase after that girl. Mack is getting the horses ready.'

Bonny skipped out to the stable-barn with Jessie in tow. 'There he is waiting for me!' She bounded up to the horse she knew so well and with whom she had a special bond. Zoro let out a soft whinny and when she approached, he gave her a gentle nudge with his head.

Jessie was just in time to see this special girl bonding with the horse in a way she hadn't witnessed before, not since seeing how Hope Rigby handled horses.

She drew alongside Mack. 'I think she has that special gift with horses that Hope Rigby has—a potential horse whisperer.'

'I think so too. That's why I brought her out here to see the musterers on their horses in action. Zoro recognised her straight away.' Mack approached Zoro and checked his saddle and girth.

'Now, Bonny—after I fasten his bridle over the halter, I'll help you mount using that mounting block over there.'

'I don't need one. I can pull myself on his back with my foot in the stirrup.'

'No, we don't do that, Bonny. It's hard on the horse's spine. I'm sure your coach, Sara taught you that.'

Bonny set her jaw and pouted.

'I've done it heaps of times when I had my own horse.'

'Please don't argue, Bonny. Here we think of caring for our horses. If you use the mounting block it takes the strain off his back. I'll lead Zoro over there and help you up.'

Jessie glanced sideways and chuckled at Mack's efforts to tame the adolescent girl as she saddled Chantilly.

Mack borrowed Walter's horse which his grandfather no longer used for mustering. Now that the ageing shepherd's riding days were over, university students who frequented the station would often ride him, or sometimes Wyatt worked the stock horse when Mack needed extra men on horseback.

Mack rode on ahead of Zoro in a single file with Chantilly behind. It was safer for Bonny this way, although Mack was sure that Zoro would do her no harm and Mack had attached a lead rope to his halter as a precautionary measure during the muster.

'I don't want to be led—you promised me I could ride Zoro by myself on the station.'

Mack glared at her. 'Not yet, Bonny. It's too dangerous to let you go yet. You're just observing at the moment. Once we are back in the paddock close to the homestead you can ride him free rein there. I'll lead Zoro just for now while you watch the musterers. The horses can get excited during mustering, so just watch for now.'

Walter was already down on the flat with the shepherds who'd brought the Merinos down from the hills. The dogs raced back and forth herding hundreds of sheep towards the bottom paddocks. Walter walked amongst them, oblivious to the clouds of dust billowing in the breeze. He used his shepherd's hook to steady himself, now and then stumbling on rough ground, but nothing seemed to thwart him once he was amongst the sheep with his own dogs.

Mack followed the muster back down to the low-lying paddocks leading Bonny all the way. He stopped to let her come alongside him.

'Why are the dogs chasing the sheep towards the woolsheds?'

'They aren't chasing them—they are rounding them up and guiding them in the right direction. Can you see the shepherds over there with their hooks?' Mack pointed to the rugged hills above them. 'They have walked all the way up there on those rocky crags to find each sheep and bring them down to the bottom. They can't take a horse up there.'

'Why do they have to go to the woolshed? Are they going to shear them?'

'They are going to crutch the ewes, which are the females. They'll remove all the discoloured wool and dags which is necessary before they give birth to their lambs.'

Mack wasn't keen to elaborate on the topic of mating to a twelve-year-old girl. 'We then leave them to graze in the paddocks surrounding the woolshed until spring when the pregnant ewes will have their lambs.'

Mack led Bonny down the track out of the way of the muster and once the stockmen had herded all the sheep, they brought them down to the woolshed. Jessie helped round up the rest of the stragglers on Chantilly.

Mack chose a paddock where the sheep would not be grazing until after spring. He dismounted next to the gate but still kept hold of Zoro's lead rope while he led Bonny through.

'Here you are. They won't be using this paddock today so you can now have free rein on Zoro for a while. Let me see what you can do.'

He unclipped the lead rope from Zoro's halter which lay underneath a well-oiled black bridle—the one Jessie had given him for Christmas the year he had proposed to her.

The look on Bonny's face said it all. She lit up like a Christmas tree as she urged Zoro first into a trot around the field then into a canter.

Mack held his breath then remembered to let it go. He trusted Zoro that he would not throw her off, but did Bonny have the balance and ability to ride a stock horse? Mack had seen her in action at Meg's in such a way to convince him she had special abilities, but he still felt the need to caution her as she pelted towards him.

He stood in front of the oncoming horse. 'Whoa!' He grabbed hold of the halter. 'Bonny, I don't want you to ride too fast. Just a gentle canter, please. Remember Zoro is my horse and you need to do as I say. I don't want any accidents while you're in my care.'

'Okay, Mr Mack, I hear you. Let me see if he can still do tricks with me—watch.'

Before Mack could assist her, she sprang off the horse and stood next to Zoro. She tied a knot in the reins, placed them on the horse's withers and walked slowly in front of him. 'Come on, Zoro—follow me.' Ambling across the paddock, she turned her head now and then to see if the horse obeyed her. Zoro loped behind following her footsteps.

As Mack gazed with astonishment, another horse approached the fence. It was Jessie who'd arrived just in time to see the unusual spectacle. They both gaped at the performing duo as Zoro followed Bonny to and fro across the paddock and back again. The girl started jogging and from time to time she checked that Zoro was in close pursuit. To Mack and Jessie's amazement, the horse followed in her footsteps trotting behind her carefully as she darted to the left and right in a zig-zag fashion. Zoro never budged an inch from walking behind, heedful not to trample her.

'This is incredible, Mack. This is your reward for your hard work at trying to help Meg and Joe. If you hadn't aided Meg in turning her life around by insisting she start a pony camp, Bonny wouldn't be here today and you would never have witnessed this. God is blessing you for being a blessing to so many others.'

'I think so, Jessie. It sure feels like providence or something.'

It was time to go. They could hear the muster approaching the woolshed. Soon the track between the paddocks would be a dusty, onslaught of barking dogs, noisy sheep, and musterers yelling at their dogs and each other.

'Let's get this young horse whisperer back to the homestead. We can't tire her all at once—there is always tomorrow.'

Chapter Twenty-One

Winter

Walter lay back in his vintage, leather armchair wriggling his toes in front of a roaring fire. His fawn, woollen socks were worse for wear. Hazel had once knitted them and each time they wore a hole, Bessie took out her needle and repaired them.

An overweight, neutered tomcat, who'd identified the pushover who often saved leftovers from the Sunday roast lamb, lay at Walter's feet.

Buster snuggled against the woollen socks that protruded close to the fire almost singeing them, while the octogenarian snored with his mouth open wide. On the opposite side of the lounge sat Jessie next to Mack, her hands moving in sequence pulling on the thick ball of wool lying on the couch next to her.

Mack picked up the wool and rolled it around in his hands. 'How's the jumper going? It looks as if it's taking shape. Pity you have to reproduce the same garment for Will. That's the only real drawback with twins—always having to double up with everything.'

'It's not that so much,' replied Jessie. 'It's just that I'm too tired to knit in the evenings after a long day running a clinic and riding on the station. I might ask Mum to do the jumper for Will, as I don't have the time. Those days are ending.'

Mack stretched out on the couch, resting his legs across Jessie's lap. 'Oh, that's a pity—just when I thought you were becoming a domesticated housewife.'

Jessie picked up a jumbo knitting needle and whacked him with it. 'Hey, none of that sexist talk—you'll never keep me in a box.'

A loud snort emanated from Walter which caused them both to erupt with laughter.

Mack stood up and reached over to a small stack of logs and placed one inside in the wood burner, while Jessie went to the kitchen to put the kettle on.

'Grandad has been sleeping so long. Do you think I should wake him? He'll be up half the night if we don't. Anyway—he always has tea at this time.'

'You could, I suppose, but do it gently. You don't want to give him a heart attack,' he teased.

Walter came to life when Jessie woke him and showed him a mug of tea and a slice of banana bread.

'You shouldn't have let me nap so long. I've been asleep for hours.'

'You must have needed it, Grandad. You spent ages in your workshop today. What are you doing out there?'

'I found some old timber to make the boys a rocking horse each for their first birthdays. It will get tricky with presents now that their birthdays are so close to Christmas.'

'That's a wonderful present to give them. They'll love them. You could call them Zoro and Chantilly—paint one black and the other gold.'

'I could do that—great idea.'

'I spoke to Meg on the phone earlier. She and Joe are getting on well. He took to the pony camp venture right off. Meg says he's right in his element,' said Mack, helping himself to a slice of banana bread.

'Pity pony camp closes down until spring in November. I don't know what Joe will do for three months, until then.'

'Meg has plenty lined up for him to do, Grandad. You know her. She has him fixing fences, feeding the horses and now he's renovating the bunkrooms before camp starts again.'

Walter laughed. 'That's Meg for you—always on the go.'

'She mentioned something I thought would give you a lift, Grandad. They want to renew their marriage vows and would like some ideas on where to do it. I said I would ask you to get in touch with her and discuss it.'

'Praise God—that sure is an answer to prayer. I'll do that—I think I have the perfect place for them.'

****

On a clear, crisp morning during a hoar frost in August, Mack and Walter ventured on an expedition to Lake Tekapo in the McKenzie country. With Meg and Joe sitting in the back of Jessie's Land Rover, they headed past Lake Wakatipu aiming to reach their destination at the Church of the Good Shepherd within five hours.

Meg and Joe were about to renew their marriage vows at the church where Walter married Hazel and where she was buried. Jessie stayed home with the twins, as she knew this should only be a Reed family affair and the trip would be too much for the babies.

As Mack drove along the Queenstown-Glenorchy highway, an orange ball of fire rose from behind the Remarkables—the mountain range opposite Lake Wakatipu. The early morning sun illuminated the feathery ice crystals formed by the hoar frost that glistened on the trees.

The vehicle meandered its way through the Lindis Valley revealing an icy wonderland. Some of the houses had their lights on illuminating the shimmering ice crystals.

Joe shivered and wrapped his arms around Meg after pulling his woollen beanie over his forehead.

'We have to be crazy doing this—it's freezing up here. Are you all right in the front, Grandad? The heating in this vehicle of Jessie's doesn't do much.'

'I'm a tough, Otago farmer—what do you expect, eh? I'm wearing my Long Johns—pure merino underwear.'

'Oh, thanks for that information, Grandad!' They all laughed.

'Doesn't it look like a fairyland down there? I've seen nothing like this before,' said Meg, fastening the woollen scarf around her neck.

Joe leaned over to pat Mack on the shoulder.

'Mack—we're ever so grateful that you offered to drive us, particularly as you're used to driving on these roads. I wouldn't like to risk driving in these treacherous conditions in unknown territory.'

Meg looked at Joe with teary eyes and sniffed. 'That's why we call him a *Good Shepherd*. In fact, both you and Grandad are just that—*Good Shepherds*. You round us up and sort us out, and you rescue and help us to heal.'

'I think we're all getting a touch sentimental. Poor Mack won't be able to stay on the road soon.' Walter chuckled.

'Grandad—during which month did you and Grandma marry at the Church of the Good Shepherd—was it winter like this?'

'It sure was. It snowed and your grandmother wanted photos taken while everything was white. I can still remember when we spotted an old, clinker dinghy upturned at the lakeside. Hazel struggled over to it in her high-heeled shoes for a photo shoot. She climbed onto the boat, dragging her wedding dress while she half froze. I might add that the photos were amazing—her long, raven-black hair against the backdrop of the Southern Alps.' Walter sat staring out the window, momentarily transported to a time past.

'I hope your rental cottage is warm, Grandad. Are you sure it's not tenanted right now?'

'I'm certain Mack. I receive updates from the Property Manager regularly. That's why I thought it a good time to do an overnighter. It's heated and has all we need. Bessie packed a full chilly bin with enough food to last until we get back late tomorrow afternoon.'

As Mack drove the vehicle with caution through to the other side of the Lindis Pass, the road opened out. When Lake Pukaki surfaced before their eyes, Walter wiped his brow with his sleeve and started sniffing, as if he was having a quiet cry—at least, that's what Mack thought as he worked hard focusing his attention on the black ice on the road while glancing sideways at Walter. Mack felt compassion for him as the battle-weary man almost reached the burial site of his beloved Hazel and the church where the two of them exchanged vows he couldn't always keep.

'Almost there, Grandad. There's Lake Pukaki. Lake Tekapo is the next one along.'

'Right you are, Mack.'

Meg and Joe sat quietly in the back. Meg had been resting her head on Joe's shoulder dozing, but when she heard that the lakes were in sight, she sat up and leaned over Walter's shoulder, her eyes scanning the view.

'Wow! Look at that lake. Just how you described it to me, Grandad. It's turquoise-blue and milky looking.'

'Yep, you won't see that in many parts of the country. It's caused by glacial flour—the silt that flows down from the glaciers.'

'It's amazing. No wonder Grandma loved growing up in these parts.'

As they passed Lake Pukaki and around the next bend in the road, Lake Tekapo boasted a similar panorama. Scattered around the lake appeared clusters of pine trees shimmering in the sunlight with the melting ice.

As they drove into Tekapo village, Walter sat wrenching his hands.

'Right, Grandad. You'll have to direct me from here. Where's this grand cottage of yours?' Mack pulled over into a recess.

'Take that turn up there on the right and travel about two miles up. You'll see a Norfolk Pine on your right in front of a little white cottage. This used to be all farmland but now it's mostly holiday homes on small lots.'

'Thanks, Grandad. I thought Grandma's parents lost everything on their farm?'

'Farming friends purchased the farm, but they left an acre of land for Hazel's folks along with their cottage out of goodwill, as they got it for a good price. After Hazel died, I rented it out. It paid for the rates bill.'

Meg turned to Joe and whispered, 'Wow, there's still a lot to learn about Grandad. I wonder what else we don't know about him. He appears to be full of surprises.'

'He sure is one special man. This is an amazing place to re-commit our lives together—I mean, Lake Tekapo.'

Meg leaned over Walter's shoulders and strained for a closer look.

'I can't wait to see this little church, Grandad. Where is it?'

'We bypassed it on the way here. It's not far, down at the lakeside. You'll see it in the morning. The Pastor is meeting you at ten o'clock. He is the grandson of the clergyman who married us—but 3let's have a meal and a good night's sleep first.'

Mack swerved as the vehicle missed a deep pothole full of water in the driveway, pulling up alongside a well-maintained cottage with leadlight windows.

Mack, Joe and Meg piled out to stretch their legs, leaving Walter in the vehicle. For a moment, he sat still taking a few deep breaths. He wiped his eyes and stepped out.

'Where's that key? Oh yes, at the side of the house you'll see the water tank. Next to that are some giant mushrooms made of clay. They have lids you can open. The red one contains the key.'

Mack raced around to the side of the house. The ice had melted and left a muddy mess on the ornamental mushrooms in the garden. He took the key forcing it into the lock, stiffened by the hoar frost.

'Come on, Grandad. You go in first.'

Walter stood back. 'No, mate—all of you can go in and choose a room. I just need to gather my thoughts first.'

Meg placed her arm around her grandfather's shoulders and pulled him close. 'Don't get cold, Grandad. It's freezing out here. We'll get the fire on, presuming you have one.'

'That's all good, lass. Away you go, then. No one can live in these parts without a good firebox. The logs are stacked next to it, just through the living room.'

They all went inside. Walter took his time wandering around the outside of the cottage, now and then folding his arms and staring at the garden where Hazel had spent hours in a day beautifying the grounds. He pulled his Swaandri up around his neck then closed his eyes and muttered—'Thank you, God, for bringing me back here, but most of all, for what I'm about to witness with my dear granddaughter at Hazel's church where it all began.'

Mack's voice drowned out the rest of Walter's prayer as he called him to join them for a light meal.

****

Heavy snow fell during the night. The next morning, as Meg opened the door, a white carpet reached the steps to greet her as she caught sight of a rabbit hopping across the front yard. She looked up at the clear, blue sky and inhaled the crisp air—catching her breath as she puffed out her chest.

Dressed only in thick, flannelette pyjamas, she shivered. Joe crept up behind her, lifted her hair from off her shoulders and kissed her neck. She reached back and caressed his face.

'Morning, love. Where are the men—have they gone out already?' she asked.

'No, not yet. Mack's still sound asleep. I knocked and opened the door. They are both dead to the world. The spare room is full to the brim with old furniture and too cluttered for anyone to sleep in, poor Mack. Grandad's snoring is terrible.'

Joe pulled her back inside the house.

'It's freezing. Didn't you bring a dressing gown?'

'No, I forgot it. I'll grab my woollen jacket from the bedroom.'

The kettle boiled, filling the kitchen with steam. Joe found a jar of coffee in the chilly bin that Bessie had packed.

Meg returned wearing a pair of thermal workmen's socks that Joe had lent her. After buttoning her jacket up to her neck, she began fossicking in the chilly bin to see what remained after the meal they ate the previous night. Removing the eggs, butter, milk, marmalade and cheese, she reached to the bottom and discovered the large chunk of half-eaten corned beef wrapped in aluminium foil. In another small package, there was homemade bread and various tins of vegetables.

She pointed at the food she'd laid out on the bench. 'This should be enough to keep us going until we get back.'

Joe joined her at the bench. 'Good! Let's tuck into those eggs—I'll make a large omelette for all of us.' His eyes smiled at her. 'You go and sit down—there's only room for one in this kitchen.'

Before long, Mack arrived with Walter dressed and ready for breakfast and the smell of eggs cooking.

He rubbed his hands together. 'Mmm—just what I need to warm my insides. It was cold in that room last night, even with the vibration of Grandad's snoring warming the air.'

Walter swiped him with his Stetson before placing it on a side table. 'I know you would rather share a room with Jessie but I'm the best offer you have at the moment.'

'Yeah well—pity the spare room is used as storage or we could have had a room each. It really needs clearing out of all that old furniture.'

Mack silently wondered when and how that would happen, as it had been like that for years—all the old furniture Hazel had kept that once belonged to her parents was dumped in one room.

They all sat at the table enjoying some of the food that Bessie had packed for them and continuing the banter until it was time to go to the church.

Mack had not seen the Church of the Good Shepherd covered in snow. He'd only visited Tekapo during the summer holidays years ago and did not know that his grandfather had a cottage there. Meg and Joe and had never seen the church either.

The setting was an artist's canvas with the snow-covered Alps forming a backdrop to the turquoise lake and stone church at the water's edge.

As they drove up to the church, they looked aghast at the wonder of it all—except for Walter who stepped out of the vehicle with a poker face and red eyes.

Meg rushed up to her grandfather and gave him a bear hug.

'Oh, what a wonderful venue for our ceremony. Thank you so much, Grandad!'

He kissed her on the cheek. 'My pleasure, my dear. It's just a pity your grandmother isn't alive to witness all of this.'

Mack reached out to him and placed a hand on his shoulder. 'Never mind, Grandad—she is with us in spirit—in our hearts. Wait—isn't that the Pastor? We'd better get on up there.'

They made their way single file up the stony path that led to the front entrance of the church. As they entered the historical building which was built by pioneers in 1935, they each shook hands with Pastor Paul.

Meg and Joe approached the altar, mesmerised by the breathtaking view of the Southern Alps through a feature window behind a large wooden cross. They turned around to view the décor of the inside of the church.

'Joe, look—there are Mum and Dad!'

Len and Helen stood under the archway at the front entrance talking to the Pastor. Helen spotted them and waved.

Meg's eyes streamed. Joe handed her a handkerchief to wipe her eyes, which she popped into her handbag.

Walter sat at the front of the church with Mack sitting next to him. Len and Helen joined them.

There wasn't a dry eye amongst them while the Pastor conducted the ceremony.

Meg had something to say at the end after coughing to clear her throat. 'Thank you all for being here for this amazing, memorable event. You have travelled a great distance and Joe and I want you to know that we'll be eternally grateful to you—but I want to especially pay homage to two people who made this happen—Mack and Grandad. You deserve your reputation as Good Shepherds who helped our family to heal and saved our marriage. So we have renewed our marriage vows at this church in honour of you both. Thank you for your long-suffering and never giving up on us.'

With that speech, more handkerchiefs came out. After the service, Meg and Joe mingled with Len and Helen. Outside the church, the men took out their cameras and Pastor Paul offered to take photos.

Meg kissed her mother. 'Thanks again for coming.'

Len, making sure he didn't miss out pulled her towards him and kissed her.

'You never mentioned to me that you planned to be here.'

Helen smiled at her daughter. 'Your brother convinced us to come and surprise you,' she said, just as Mack approached and greeted his parents in the same way.

'Where are you staying?' Mack asked. 'You know we could have arranged accommodation if you hadn't insisted on being independent.'

'It wasn't a problem, honestly. We're in the Lakeside Motel. It's pretty basic, but all we need. We weren't sure whether to book another night,' said Len.

'Are you still going to follow us to Glenorchy? You weren't sure when I telephoned.' Mack glanced at his wristwatch.

Meg turned to her parents. 'What's all this? Our guesthouse is empty for the rest of the winter so you can stay with us and spend time visiting your grandchildren.'

Helen glanced at Joe. 'Don't you two need to be alone—I mean—it's your honeymoon?'

He laughed. 'We've had all the honeymoons we need, haven't we?'

Meg elbowed him. 'Our chalet will soon be vacant, as Charlie, our caretaker is retiring.'

Len's brows furrowed. 'Oh! What will you do then?'

'I don't know. I'll have Joe to help me with pony camp, but there's so much to do around the property. We'll have to advertise for someone to replace him.'

Mack jerked his thumb at them, 'Let's go back to the cottage for lunch. We can discuss it over a meal. We've plenty of tucker with us. We just have to leave in time to travel in the light. It'll take five hours in these wintery conditions to get back and even then, I advise caution on these roads.'

Walter took hold of Len's arm. 'Wait, all of you! I need to do something before we go back. I want to show Mack and Meg where their grandmother is buried.'

'Of course, Dad. They haven't been here before and I came down here a few years ago. Shall we all go?' Len took the lead with the entourage in tow.

Meg looked searchingly for the multi-coloured lupins that Walter often spoke about that grew alongside the lake, but there was no sign of them.

'No lupins to put on Grandma's grave. What can I put there, Grandad?'

'No, lassie—not in this snow. Lupins won't appear until November when it's warmer.'

Walter pulled a compact bouquet of dark-red, dried roses from the pocket of his navy-blue woollen Peacoat and handed it to her.

'Here, you can place that on her gravestone.'

Mack, Len and Helen walked behind them and watched Meg while she placed the flowers on the grave. They bowed their heads while Walter prayed and after he'd finished, they stood for a moment in silence. Walter's face had lost its gaunt appearance and his facial lines softened.

He smiled as he removed from his pocket a small wooden, hand-carved cross he'd made and placed it on the gravestone.

'All is well with the world, Lord,' he muttered quietly.

Chapter Twenty-Two

'Guess what.' Mack snuggled up to Jessie in front of the fire, revelling in the stillness. Walter and Bessie had already turned in early.

'My folks surprised Meg by turning up at the ceremony. They talked about leaving Nelson and moving into the chalet at Willow Park now that Meg's caretaker is retiring. Mum wants to spend more time with her grandsons. They said they've missed out on seeing them growing up, although they aren't a year old yet.'

'That's marvellous. You'll have your whole family down here just as I do, except for Tom and he won't be leaving the farm in Bethlehem. I wonder how he and Amanda are getting on. I thought he said they were looking at getting married next spring, but we've heard nothing about it.'

'You know your brother. He's just as likely to change his mind. Maybe they need longer.'

'It's a pity you weren't at the ceremony, Jessie. I felt bad leaving you behind.'

'You know we couldn't take the twins on such a long trip. It would have been chaotic and too cold in that cottage. I'm sure Meg and Joe understood.'

'Well, thanks for holding the fort while we were away.'

'I've got a big day at the clinic tomorrow. There are two dogs that need neutering, and that Scotsman, McKlintoch on the deer farm has a young buck that is lame. He thinks it may have injured itself trying to get through a fence. He's bringing it down to the bus in his horse truck when I'm in Kinloch this afternoon.'

Mack flicked his wrist to see the time. 'I'll ask my mother to help your mum with the boys. She'd planned on visiting us tomorrow—sorry, I forgot to tell you. She's so keen to see them.'

'That's a great idea—I'll phone my mother and let her know to expect her. We've got so much support now, we're so blessed.'

'I also forgot to tell you—Meg and Joe are coming with us to church this Sunday and so are Mum and Dad. They're putting on a morning tea to celebrate their reconciliation.'

'Great news! Come on, Mack. The fire's almost out. Let's go to bed. I don't get to spend much time with you these days.'

He turned out the lights and led her down the hallway. It was Jessie's turn to receive a portion of her husband's love that seemed to overflow from his heart, the kind that served as a catalyst for change in the lives of so many.

Tonight Mack would sleep peacefully knowing that everything in his world seemed right. Not only had his grandfather made peace with himself and his family, but Meg had also finally redeemed herself.

****

The first day of spring arrived. Hope Rigby stood at the gate with baby Sophie and her brother, Bertie waving as Jessie arrived. Bertie ran to the car and banged on the window as she turned off her engine.

He pointed at his sister. 'Look, Sophie can walk—see!' He grabbed Jessie's hand almost pulling her over as she stepped out of the car.

Hope took his hand and moved him aside. 'Hold on, Bertie. Wait until Aunty Jessie gets the boys out of the back seat.'

Jessie unclipped each child from their car seats and let them toddle onto the grass while she reached out and hugged her friend.

'It's so long since we've caught up. I'm dying to hear all your news.' Hope lifted Sophie and coaxed Bertie up the steps with Jessie in tow with her boys.

'It's such a beautiful spring day—I love this season. Let's have tea on the veranda in the sun while the children play on the grass.

It's dry now, and the garden is fenced off so we can watch them from here.'

Hope hurried back with a tray of tea and cake. She showed Jessie small pieces of fruit, and homemade bread covered in peanut butter, cut into squares.

'Okay if your boys share this with Sophie and Bertie?'

'Absolutely—go ahead.'

Hope walked down the steps with a blanket to spread on the grass, followed by Jessie who placed the plate of fruit and bread down. The two sat drinking English Breakfast tea while sampling Hope's freshly baked banana cake.

Hope's face appeared animated. 'We haven't done this since we were both pregnant. How time goes by so fast—now tell me all the juicy stuff.'

'Well, you know about Grandad's earlier estrangement with his entire family. There has been a miraculous healing and they are reunited. As well as all that, Meg and Joe are back together again for good.'

'My goodness—how did all that come about?'

'First of all, it was Mack who brought the family completely back together and healed their relationship. He has been amazing—so compassionate and insightful for a high country farmer. That makes me love him even more. He prayerfully intervened and through his persistence and wise words, he never gave up. He convinced Meg her marriage was worth saving and just how selfish she'd been. Grandad also had an enormous impact on Meg by confessing to her what a rotter he'd been to Grandma. He had neglected her after she gave birth to Len and her health deteriorated as a result of his selfishness.'

'That's unbelievable. What a turnaround!'

'To add to that, Grandad has let go of his self-hatred of not taking care of Grandma. They are such different people now. Please thank your family for all their prayers. I'll have to tell our church prayer chain, too.'

'That's no problem. You would have done the same for us.'

'Oh-oh! Sophie's trying to pull her nappy off. I don't like to think what's inside it. She does that if it needs changing—if you know what I mean.' She walked off with Sophie while Jessie wiped peanut butter off the twins' faces. In a short time, Hope returned with her daughter tucked under one arm.

Jessie pointed to Bertie. 'I can't believe how much he has grown. How is kindergarten going—has the class increased in size much?'

'He loves it but the class is too big. They need another classroom and they still only have one teacher.'

'Is it still part of the little school?'

'Yes, and it's too small for all the children coming into the area. A developer has built a large subdivision on the Closeburn side of Glenorchy—mostly families live there.'

'Yes, I see that. I think that's the property developer who wanted to buy land from Meg. It's a tragedy.'

'I agree—they're an eyesore—houses made of ticky-tacky.'

'Jessie—I was wondering if Meg is ready for me to come and help with the horses. I did promise—remember? I no longer have classes at Dart River Ranch, and I kind of miss it.'

'I'm sure she'll appreciate your offer, but pony camp doesn't start until November when summer begins. You could help her train the new ponies, as they need some groundwork. Perhaps you had better call her.'

'I sure will. Thanks, Jessie—that'll be right up my alley. Mum has offered to babysit so I can get out a few days a week now.'

'You're like me—you have built-in babysitters. I'm so lucky that I'll have two lots with Mack's parents having moved down from Nelson to Willow Park and absolutely loving it. Meg's caretaker has retired so they now live in the chalet that Meg built for my parents.'

'Jeepers! Major changes going on with your family but all good, though.'

'How about you—how is the breeding program going? Are you still involved now you have two children?'

'It's doing well—only it has quietened down now as the mating season is over and most of our mares are pregnant. Cole has taken on an assistant, as Dad is pulling back and giving him more responsibility. I work a few days a week with Cole and sometimes I get requests to break in a local horse.'

'You're like me—employed both inside and outside the home. We're tough women.'

'Cole has to call on the services of the on-call vet to carry out the pre-pregnancy checks on the mares, but next season he would like you do conduct them.'

'Jeepers! I'm going to be busy, aren't I?'

'We can't let you off lightly.'

'Sorry, Hope. I must take the boys home for their afternoon nap. They'll be getting grumpy soon. Don't forget to give Meg a call about helping out with her ponies.'

'I will do. Come on, boys, I'd better get you home.'

She gathered the twins one by one and bustled them into their car seats.

'Thanks for the tea and that lovely banana cake—you haven't lost your knack.' She gave Hope a warm hug, climbed in her vehicle, and drove off tooting all the way up the driveway.

****

Jessie startled awake next morning to her alarm screaming at her on the bedside table. Mack's side of the bed was empty. He appeared in the doorway holding grizzling baby Oliver.

'Don't worry, he's had his breakfast.' Mack handed him to his mother for a cuddle.

Jessie slid into her slippers. 'I was going to get up and let you have a sleep in—that's why I set the alarm. I get more time to take breaks than you do. Why don't you go back to bed? I'll watch the boys.'

She knew that the start of the lambing season was tough for Mack. He'd been hard at it since daybreak each day checking all the ewes that they had brought down to the valley during the last muster. He found a few of them cast—weighed down by their weight because of the lush green grass after the spring rain. The sheep were heavy to lift onto their feet once they were on the ground.

Mack crawled back under the blankets. 'Thanks, love. I'll just lie here for a while and relax.'

What he usually meant by that was pray. But this time, unwanted thoughts crowded God out. He knew that before long it would be Jessie's turn to be out on the station using her veterinary expertise to assist him with difficult births. The Angus cows are another story and Jessie will have her work cut out when calving begins. The thought of their overwhelming workload caused him to pull the covers over his head and blank out, even for a short time. Sometimes he thought he'd bitten off more than he could chew when he took the job over from his grandfather but now there was no turning back.

She was right—her mother gave her sufficient breaks from the boys and she didn't do full days on the station, although she was also a station manager. When Mack married Jessie, she took over the book-keeping from Walter. Now it was time to employ a bookkeeper with her trying to manage three part-time jobs, Mack said to himself. That'll be the next thing on the agenda—unless Wyatt would like to do it.

Jessie wandered down the hallway with Oliver after checking that Will was still asleep in the nursery.

Mack lay back, engulfed by the resonating stillness of the dawn. The buzzing of cicadas invaded his peace—or was it his tinnitus, the one characteristic he knew he'd inherited from his grandfather that occurred when he was tired or pressured.

Before long, a child's whimper in the next room shattered his oblivion. Should he jump out of bed and hurry to him? At once the sound of Jessie's soft voice interrupted the whine and then there was silence. Mack's body forced him to stay motionless. He deserved a day off.

Mid-morning he rose and freshened up in the bathroom ready to take on the world again. Bessie had set them a simple breakfast and was out at the henhouse collecting eggs.

Jessie had Will in his highchair while Oliver sat playing on a rug on the floor. She scooped a large dollop of strawberry jam from the glass jar and spread it on her toast.

'There's still porridge in the pot if you want some. If you are going to eat toast, would you mind popping a couple more slices in the toaster?' she asked, licking her fingers.

'I'll give the porridge a miss this morning. I tend to go off it in the warm weather. That's a fresh pot of strawberry jam, isn't it? I saw Bessie making it yesterday.'

They sat chatting over coffee and toast, revelling in Bessie's jam while still in their pyjamas.

'Grandad's sleeping late. I hope he's alright. He's been getting a few bad headaches again.'

'I wouldn't worry about it—at his age, he's bound to slow down. He's coming up eighty-six.'

Jessie unclipped the safety strap in Will's highchair and placed him on the rug next to Oliver.

'He's unbelievable—still riding his quad bike and repairing fences after having two strokes. Strong stock, the Reed family. I hope you and the boys inherit his longevity.'

'I forgot to tell you I dropped by to see Meg on my way back from the Feed Depot. They have decided to let the rooms out in the guesthouse to tourists until Christmas and start pony camp after the New Year during the school holidays. Joe has purchased a new vehicle to offer tourists mini-tours of the area and they have travel agents in Queenstown doing some promotion.'

'Gosh. What brought this on?'

'It's a great way for them to make extra income during the winter. He may continue the tours when pony camp is on, but the guesthouse will be only used for the children at that time so they'll just be day tours.'

Jessie pushed the double baby stroller into the lounge. 'That's a great idea. It looks like it's all falling into place for them—oh, I just remembered our horses still have their covers on and it's going to be a warm day today.'

'I'll take care of it as I've got to do my rounds of the pregnant animals. I'll be taking Zoro out, but I'll take Chantilly's cover off first.'

'Your folks will be arriving soon and your Mum wants to babysit. I can do the covers later.'

'That will be a great help. So good to have them living nearby on Meg's property instead of in Nelson.'

Jessie stroked Mack's hair and kissed him.

He cupped her face in his hands. 'It's as if God had planned it all—everything that has taken place up to now can't just be a coincidence—in fact, I no longer believe in that. It has to be divine intervention. We have been truly blessed, Jessie.' He kissed her again and walked off.

Chapter Twenty-Three

Mack wandered off down the track that led to the horses' paddocks. Chantilly and Zoro shared grazing together while Walter's horse, an old gelding was kept in his stable, as he, like Walter, was the veteran on the station. The stockmen kept their horses in another paddock on the other side of the stable-barn.

'What is it, buddy?' He looked around him and took a deep breath. Is it the stench of smoke? Probably someone burning off crop stubble, he decided.

He took the cover off both horses and put the halter with lead rope on Zoro. Chantilly pig-jumped and put her ears back. Mack knew she was annoyed he was taking Zoro out and not her.

'Don't worry, girl. Your turn's coming soon. Zoro has some work to do.'

He led his horse out of the paddock checking behind him that Chantilly didn't try to bolt through the gate. Within minutes he arrived at the stable-barn where he saddled and bridled Zoro.

'Come on, buddy. Let's go see where this smoke is coming from—just in case.'

He could see plumes of thick, black smoke in the distance but needed to get high up where he could view the surrounding area as he rode up onto a steep ridge.

His heart sank as his eyeballs widened like glass marbles. He removed his Stetson and swished his fingers back through his hair replacing the hat. The billows of smoke loomed high above his neighbour, Ned's barn.

'Walk on.' Mack wanted to race down but knew that one hasty step too many, horse and rider would roll to the bottom of the craggy hillside.

Once down on the flat, he urged Zoro into a canter back down the track to their stable-barn. Once there, after quickly removing his harness, he let him go inside his pen.

Mack rushed up to the homestead yelling out to Jessie, tripping up the steps on his way into the living room.

'Quick, phone the fire brigade. Ned's barn's on fire—I'll see if I can help.'

Jessie raced to the phone. 'Please be careful, love. You have baby boys—remember!'

Mack charged out of the house before Jessie finished her sentence and jumped into his Ute driving like a madman onto the main road. The vehicle rattled his bones as he hurtled along the loose metal road for the five-minute drive to Ned's before careering into his driveway. A cat darted in front of his wheels and into a bush.

Mack torpedoed over to the barn where layers of heavy smoke surged through the roof window. He held a handkerchief to his face as he arrived at the entrance calling out to Ned. His stomach somersaulted when he heard the shrill neigh of a horse in the corner of the barn, but as he glanced above him, he was relieved to see that the fire was still in the roof and hadn't reached the floor of the barn.

'Ned!' he screamed as he looked around, but the intense crackling of the fire raged through the wooden framework of the roof and drowned his voice.

Mack approached the horse whose ears were erect, tipping forwards while his nostrils flared. He danced around the pen throwing his head up and down whinnying, his tail swishing furiously.

Mack grabbed a lead rope hanging from a hook near the horse that now reared, his eyes bulging, rolling backwards exposing the whites.

Mack pulled back, holding onto the rope. 'Whoa, it's okay—I'll get you out of here.'

The clip on the lead rope found its home as Mack fastened it to the halter. 'Come on, Clover, you'll have to trust me.'

Yanking off his sweatshirt, he tied it around the petrified horse's head to cover his eyes and led him out the door. Trying to keep up as Clover trotted briskly alongside him, he coaxed the horse into the open until they were out of danger. Spotting an empty paddock nearby, Mack removed his sweatshirt from the horse, opened the gate and released him. The animal whinnied and took off across the paddock bucking madly.

Mack could hear dogs whining nearby and knew they weren't in the barn but he wanted to make sure they were safe too. His throat seized with the stress of it all and dense smoke penetrated his airways causing him to gag. Running towards Ned's house he felt a deep sense of impending doom, concerned that the old man had not come out to investigate. Perhaps he had passed out in the barn overcome by smoke. Mack sprinted towards the house passing metal kennels with two sheepdogs on the way. Storming through the front door of the bungalow which was unlocked, there was Ned snoring in his armchair with his feet propped up on a leather ottoman.

Mack held back tears of relief. Ned didn't even startle at the shrill sound of sirens outside the house.

'Ned, wake up—Ned!' The farmer cringed as he woke suddenly to see a tall, muscular young man towering over him.

'What—what's this? What are you going in here, Mack?'

'Your barn's on fire—hurry! Are there any other animals in there? I got your horse out safely.'

'Clover—good heavens, man. No, there aren't any animals except for him. Where is he now?'

'I let him go in the paddock to the west of the barn. He may need some water if there's no trough.'

'Yes, there's water there. Was he hurt?'

'He's just shaken up, but I'll check on him again. The firemen are coming around the side of the house to see where they can bring the fire-engines to the fire. You'd best go and assist them right now.'

Mack left the firemen in Ned's hands and went back to check on Clover. He sidled up to him and patted him on the neck. The horse's whole body quivered.

'You're alright now, Clover. That was a close shave, wasn't it?'

He left the horse to continue grazing and wandered over to the barn which was under siege. Mack prayed silently that the fire would not destroy the whole barn, and when he arrived at the inferno, the firemen were hard at work with their hoses. He was relieved to see they had saved the external framework of the barn, apart from the roof which was severely damaged and started collapsing.

Ned leaned on his John Deere tractor parked near the fire-engines, watching the disaster unfold before him as he surveyed the wreckage.

'Can I go over, now that they have finished hosing? I need to see what's left of all my equipment and machinery,' he asked a fireman.

'You can only look from a distance, sorry, mate. For safety regulations, we can't allow you to enter the building until the fire chiefs have certified it safe to do so.'

Ned stood up when he saw Mack approach him.

'How did you know the barn was on fire? If it wasn't for you, I would have lost Clover and my house. I have little stock left now as I'm retired except for a handful of sheep up the back of the farm. It's all I have left at this time of life, including my working dogs.'

'I was riding up on the hillside to see if there were any stray sheep or cattle and saw clouds of smoke. I wouldn't have seen it from down below.' Mack guessed it must have been fate that he rode up onto the ridge to view his property at that moment.

'Well, I'm indebted to you, mate and won't forget it—I'll repay you, somehow.'

'I'm not worried about that, Ned. Seeing you are so shaken up, perhaps you'd like to come and stay with me and my family for a few days.'

Ned patted him on the back. 'There's no need for all that—thanks, anyway. I need to make sure Clover's doing alright as he'll be in shock, and I have my dogs to take care of. You're a good man and I hope this community appreciates having someone like you in their midst. You're a Godsend.'

Mack could see there was nothing else for him to do there. He would rather have Ned accompany him to Reed Station but he could see the man was stubborn and reluctant to leave. The firemen were still busy cleaning up the debris from the roof that had caved in. Tomorrow he will return to check on him.

Chapter Twenty-Four

It was supposed to be Jessie's day off, but this was one of the busiest days on the station since lambing and calving had commenced. She had to deliver intravenous fluids and oxygen to calves whose mothers had suffered difficult labour.

After Jessie finished treating the needy animals, she went home for a break and left Wyatt in the barn to watch over the calves and their mothers. She would only need to be on standby if there were complications with any of the animals.

Mack came into the house for lunch, unaccustomed to his children not bowling him over the moment they saw him appear. 'Where are the boys?'

'They're next door with my folks. Mum and I decided they are now old enough to hang out at her house when she is babysitting. She and dad have been busy setting the place up so it is safe for them to rattle around there.'

'That's great, but it doesn't matter whose house they are in as long as they don't come to any harm. When they're older, my folks might have them stay with them too, at Willow Park.'

When they had finished lunch together, Jessie started folding a pile of nappies. 'What's on your schedule for this afternoon?'

'If you don't mind, I'd like to pop over to see Ned and see if he's okay after the fire. Joe also asked if I'd drop by to see his new off-road Jeep Wagoneer. He bought one of those Sports Utility Vehicles ... SUV they're called. It even has wood grain along the side.'

'That sounds posh. What does he want with that?' Jessie said, frowning.

'Remember I told you Joe wants to start a side business taking tourists on mini-tours? The area looks spectacular during winter.'

'I think that's a clever idea and Joe needs a job. He's too young to put out to pasture. I'll stay here in case the stockmen need me with my medical bag. Let Ben know, seeing he's second in charge when we aren't around.'

'It's just that I think Joe might need a bit of support until he settled into the community. I'll take my radiophone and if you need me, call me.' Mack kissed her on his way to the door.

'I'll try to be back as soon as possible. Wyatt is pretty clued up and so are Ben and Coran. You should manage alright with them.'

****

Mack chuckled to himself watching Meg and Joe trudging around the stable yard in gumboots and overalls mucking out.

Meg looked up and leaned on her shovel—her wispy hair dishevelled by the southerly breeze.

'Mack! Good to see you—just in time to help us shift dung.'

Mack's eyes shot daggers at her until he burst out laughing, realising she was teasing.

'I was hoping for a cup of tea if you can spare the time.'

'We sure can,' said Joe. 'I'm dying for a break.'

They arrived on the porch and yanked off their boots by the front door.

Meg passed them both in the lounge. 'I'll put the kettle on,'

Joe pointed to a seat. 'Come on in and sit down. It's been a while since we caught up.'

Meg brought tea and biscuits through, served it to them and joined Joe on the couch.

'Excuse the old throw rug. We always sit here to protect our furniture when we are in our dirty work clothes.'

For the next hour, Joe told Mack about his business plan with his new vehicle, and now and then Meg managed to get a word in to ask about Jessie and the boys.

She passed the biscuits around again. 'You'll have to bring the twins to visit us soon. It's been ages since we saw them last.'

'To be honest it's probably easier for you both to come to us. It's a bit of a performance visiting with the boys as they still need a midday nap, and we can only take them out in short bursts,' said Mack.

Joe sat rubbing his hands together, eager to get back outside.

'When you've finished your tea, I'd like to show you the Wagoneer.'

Mack sat scanning the living room. 'You've updated your wallpaper. It looks much more appealing.'

Meg stood up pointing upstairs. 'And all the other rooms too. You must take a look at the guest rooms, Mack. We've also put in new bathrooms at both ends of the corridor.'

'Sure, I'll do that first and then I'll go and see Joe's new vehicle.'

Joe fidgeted in his seat looking at his watch. He stayed in the living room while Meg showed her brother around.

While Mack surveyed the renovations to the building, Meg pulled him aside. 'I want to tell you something while you're here,' she whispered. 'It's about Joshua.'

He grimaced. 'You mean that doctor friend of yours—I thought that was all finished with!'

'Shh! It's all finished—I saw him in town the other day holding hands with his new fiancée. He's marrying a nurse colleague from Tekapo and apparently, they've been friends for years. He was keen to marry her before he arrived here, but she wasn't ready. She obviously is now.'

'How do you know all this?'

'One of my friends from the Country Women's Institute knows her family in Tekapo.'

'So—how did you feel when you saw him holding her hand?'

'That's just the point—I felt nothing—in fact, it was a relief to see he has someone. I realised then that I was never in love with him and how grateful I am that Joe is back.'

'Why did you fraternise with the doctor in the first place, if that's the case?'

'When Joe stayed away, I came to believe he didn't love me or want me back.'

Mack put his arm around Meg. 'Goes to show how fickle the human mind is and how assumptions can mess up our lives. Let's get back to Joe—he'll be wondering where we've got to.'

When they walked down the stairs, they bumped into Joe who was about to come looking for them.

'Goodness! That took a long time. Talk about the grand tour. Can we go outside now and take a look at my new venture?'

Meg cleared up their cups while she gave Joe space to be with Mack.

The men pulled their boots on and wandered out to the oversized garage at the entrance to the property.

'I keep this here locked up with Meg's car.'

'Brand new, is it?' Mack stood with his eyes popping out, staring at Joe's new find. 'Superb! It even has woodgrain along the sides. Where did you come across this one?'

'That new importer, Gibson and Son in Queenstown. Take a look at the upholstery—it's all leather.'

Mack climbed into the back of the car, gliding his hand along the seats.

'Stunning! Your tourists are going to get a ride and a half in one of these. I wouldn't mind being a passenger being driven around myself.'

'Maybe we can all go on a test run out to Paradise. We can see Earnslaw there covered with snow.'

'I'm up for that—although I feel a bit guilty Jessie missing out and I'm sure she'd love to come, but she needs to stay at the station in case her medical expertise is needed. I don't want to be away too long, though.'

'Maybe Jessie can have a ride another time when she's free,' said Joe.

'I hoped to drop by the chalet to see my folks before I head back later too.'

'They've gone into Queenstown for the day. I'll tell them you called in.'

Mack was grateful his mother-in-law lived on their property. When his own mother was not available to take care of the twins, Pru was always a backstop.

****

Meg peered through the window at the spring flowers on the side of the road—a technicolour of lupins—pink, blue and purple.

Sitting in the backseat, Mack stared out at Mount Alfred as they passed the snow-capped mountain that towered over the extensive farmland. He recalled the time when he first fell in love with his wife—the time when Hope and Cole had invited him and Jessie to walk up the icy bush track to the mountain summit. Though all of them were seasoned rock climbers, Jessie slipped and fell into a deep ice-filled crevice. At the thought of her dying, Mack realised he was smitten and after he bravely rescued her, a romance blossomed.

Unexpectedly, Joe pulled up for a moment in front of a river ford.

'The water level is higher than usual. I don't like taking vehicles through water but this one is high off the ground so I don't mind.'

They arrived at a lookout point where tourists can view Mount Earnslaw. Joe pointed towards a grassy hillock. 'That's where I'll take them—up there on that hill. There's a clear view of Mt Earnslaw from there.'

'Where else will you take them?' Mack rolled down his window to take a look at the view.

'Meg has made friends with some of the station owners here and at Kinloch who've invited me to conduct tours of their farms.'

Mack raised his eyebrows. 'That's good you've made a few friends around here. They must be pretty chummy with you to extend that kind of hospitality.'

'Some of their children have attended holiday camps here to give the parents a break. Our business set up impresses them, so I guess they want to do me a favour.'

Mack reflected on how far his sister had come socially when initially she had the whole community against her. Now they go out of their way to help her.

'I'd better get back, if you don't mind, Joe. I promised Jessie I wouldn't be too long, in case she is needed in the lambing shed.'

'Sure, no problem. Just enjoy being driven around for once—let's go.'

****

When Mack arrived back at Reed Station, Jessie appeared in the driveway. Concerned, he wound down his window. 'Everything alright, love?'

'The boys are fine, but I'm needed in the lambing shed again. One of them which has a complicated presentation and is exhausted. Ben has been with her for two hours.'

'I'll go and collect the boys from your mother.'

'No, don't worry—she is happy to have them for a little longer. They are home now and Mum is inside with them. You need to take me to the ewe on the quad bike. I'll go inside first and radio Ben to let him know we're on our way.'

'Bring the radiophone back with you.'

Chapter Twenty-Five

Jessie took off inside the house for her medical bag and hurried back down the steps to climb on the bike behind Mack.

'I've got the radiophone inside my bag. Ben's waiting by the shed.'

Mack revved the engine, taking off up the track to the shed where Ben stood with his radiophone, holding open the gate.

'I'm sure glad to see you!' he said, flashing a smile at Jessie. I think this will be a prolonged labour—we've got her in the shed lying on hay.'

Jessie scrambled off the quad bike with her bag and followed Ben who carried a bucket of clean water and placed it on the ground next to her. 'Do you need soap?'

'No, thanks—I always carry my own.'

After washing her hands and arms, she took a clean hand towel from her bag to dry off and pulled on long gloves.

Mack knelt next to Jessie. 'You can see to the rest of them, Ben. I'll stay and assist Jessie.'

'Right, you are. I'll get off then.'

Jessie examined the ewe while Mack stood by to help when needed. Within minutes, the lamb's face showed.

'This is no good. I'll have to slide its head back inside and see if I can get the legs into the canal so she can deliver normally. Help me get the ewe onto her side, Mack.'

She took a thick piece of cord from her bag. After changing her gloves, she covered the lamb's head with lubricant and slid the loop of cord over the head, behind its ears and through its mouth.

'I'll ease the head back and grab hold of its legs ... wait ... here it comes.'

Before long, the lamb slid onto the hay. Mack removed the cord snare from its neck then cleared its mouth with his finger and lay the tiny creature on its side. He squeezed its ribcage a few times when he saw that its chest was barely moving and within minutes it was breathing on its own. Mack turned the ewe's head towards the limp bunch of wet fluff lying in front of the depleted mother and lifted the lamb placing it under her nose. 'She looks like a stunned mullet—not too interested yet.'

'You would be like that too! Labour is a strenuous business—that I do know—she'll come right soon.'

After the ewe had finished licking and cleaning the lamb, Jessie cut the umbilical cord and treated it with iodine to prevent infection, while Mack checked the ewe's udder before she started feeding.

After a short time, this worn-out vet was ready to go home. She rinsed and dried her hands before closing her bag. 'Are we finished here then?'

'Yep, we sure are. I'll take you home and then come back and check on her.'

'Tell the others to keep an eye on this lamb. If she appears cold and weak, I may have to give her an injection of dextrose.'

'I'll let Ben know. He may need some help with some of the other ewes as it's getting late in the day. He and Coran will be taking turns monitoring them, but they should know by their last visit at eleven tonight whether any of them will birth in the night.'

Mack pulled her close to him and glanced at her face.

'I'm so blessed to have married you, young lady. Who would have thought I'd have my own ready-made vet on a high country station?'

He kissed her and let it linger. 'When lambing is over, I'll see if Wyatt and Ben can hold the fort one weekend. They'll have Coran here too. If our parents can babysit, we could go to Queenstown and stay the night in one of those cabins by the lake you keep telling me about.'

Jessie climbed on the back of the bike. 'I'd love that. It has been a long while since we had any time together on our own. Let's plan it soon.'

To their delight, Pru had given the boys their evening meal. She'd taken them back to her house and raked up some of the meals that Bessie had pre-prepared and placed in mini containers in the fridge.

'Hope you don't mind but they are all watered and fed. I've also changed their nappies a few minutes ago. I thought you would be tied up with the ewe for ages and the boys were getting hungry.'

Jessie threw her arms around her mother.

'Oh, Mum. What would we do without you? I'm sure Mack's mother would do the same but to have you right on our doorstep is a Godsend.'

'Enough of that—Bessie dropped by and lent a hand, bless her. Do you want a hand to bath them?'

'No, I'll be okay. Mack and I can manage that together. I must remember to thank Bessie later.'

Pru helped fasten the boys in their double stroller. Before Jessie walked back home, she hesitated.

'Oh yes, I forgot to tell you—we've received a wedding invitation from Tom with short notice that they're getting married in a month! He said he sent one to you and Dad and will phone you.'

Pru raised her eyebrows a few times and chuckled.

'Typical, of Tom though—always leaving everything until last when we all live so far away. He just doesn't think—poor Amanda will have her work cut out for her.'

'I guess so, Mum, but perhaps he has a lot on his mind. I understand that, trying to run this station with Mack. It's so much responsibility.'

'You forget that when your father and I started out on our farm, we had no help from anyone. Wyatt's father was dead, and we were as green as grass. My parents lived miles away.'

'Maybe that's why it could be a challenge for Tom as he's so used to having Dad on the farm and now he has to stand on his own two feet. Anyway—regarding the wedding—from what he has said to me, Amanda wasn't interested in a formal wedding at all. She just wants a small, local church ceremony with family and a few friends and then a casual celebration back at the house.'

'He said nothing like that to me. Oh well, let's wait and see what transpires. I'll see you tomorrow, love.'

After she arrived home, Jessie gathered up the boys for their bath and found Mack already busy filling it.

They chatted while the twins played in the water.

'We must organise our trip to the Bay of Plenty for Tom's wedding next month. Did you see our invitation on the table?'

Mack tossed a rubber duck to Oliver while Will splashed around, drenching Mack's face.

'Could you pass the towel please?'

He wiped his face dry and then replied. 'You mean organising staff to run this place while we're gone. We can't rely on Grandad—he's not in a good state to leave him all the responsibility, but Ben and Coran should be able to manage. Bessie and Grandad can look after each other and I might ask Joe and Meg to visit, just to monitor things.'

'We'd best go to Queenstown this weekend and book our flights. We could look for their wedding present while we are there.'

'Good stuff. Let's get these fellas out—they're starting to shiver.'

****

They all crammed into Jessie's spacious Land Rover. The trip took a good hour going to the Queenstown Airport to catch the flights to Rotorua Airport. They left their vehicle in the secure carpark until their return and had plenty of time before the flight as they'd arrived early.

Mack dreaded taking the twins on the plane. What if they cried the whole time or messed their nappies? He detested the way they packed them in on small aircraft like dried figs in a tin. He couldn't wait to arrive.

A pretty hostess offered to help during the trip to entertain the babies during the three-hour flight that seemed to take forever for Mack.

When they arrived, Jessie and Pru changed the twins in the child-friendly bathroom at the air terminal. Wyatt and Mack waited for them at the carousel. After they all found their luggage, Mack and Jessie carried one child each in a back baby carrier.

'We should have brought their twin pushchair, Jessie,' said Pru, eyeing the weight on her daughter's back.

'No, Mum—it's cumbersome and takes up too much space. It's best this way.'

Pru knew better than to contradict her daughter who was the epitome of stubbornness.

'There he is!' Jessie waved out to Tom in the arrival lounge.

'Oh, no.' She eyed the ginger tufts of hair protruding from her brother's chin. 'It makes him look like an old man,' Jessie tittered.

They all greeted each other with a hug.

'No Amanda, Tom?' uttered Jessie, looking around him.

'No—she'll catch up with us later. She works on a Friday.'

The road trip to Tauranga from Rotorua crammed into Tom's Ford Falcon was not so bad as it could fit an army. Mack usually found it a nightmare taking the twins on such a long trip but the vehicle was comfortable. The toddlers slept for half of the journey fastened in rear side-facing bench seats, already fitted by the neighbour.

Mack tapped Tom on the shoulder. 'Cool number, this vehicle, Tom. All decked out for a large family. I've been looking forward to seeing it.'

He whispered to Jessie, 'I think he's planning on having a tribe of children,' and winked at her.

Wyatt jumped in before Tom could answer. 'Yep, it was a good buy. Pru and I thought it a handsome gift—a way of saying thank you for taking over the management of our farm.'

'And what a wonderful job he is doing too,' Pru added.

'This is superb, Tom. Is this the vehicle you managed to score from old farmer Henderson—the one you've had your eye on for years?' quizzed Jessie, trying not to throw up in the back of the car each time the vehicle veered around the deep bends in the road. She leaned her head out the window as the green rolling hills of home became clear. 'Man, I didn't realise how much I've missed this. Still—life has to go on.'

Tom turned his head sideways. 'You know you can always come and stay for a bit but you never take me up on the offer.'

'Dear Tom—if only you knew how tight my schedule is now we have twins. I'm working three jobs—and I can't just up sticks with two babies!'

Just at that moment, the vehicle hit a deep pothole in the long driveway that led to the farmhouse.

'Sorry about that—I heard you, Jessie, and believe me—I understand. Here we are, back home.'

****

The quaint, white-washed chapel started filling with the bridal party, families and friends. It was the size of the one in Glenorchy, a small historic building.

Pru checked Jessie's hat, attempting to tuck loose strands of hair away. 'It's a perfect summer's day. Tom couldn't have asked for anything better than this. Do I look alright—is my collar lying flat?'

'Don't fuss, mother. It's fine. Where are Dad and Mack? We had better go in and sit down.'

Before they entered the chapel, Jessie stopped to smell the gardenia bush that featured by the entrance to the church.

'Jessie!' Pru whispered, 'You can't pick those.'

Jessie frowned at her mother. 'I'm not picking them—I haven't smelled them in years.'

'Let's go inside—the men have gone in already.'

Mack and Wyatt sat together on the groom's side of the church with their wives next to them. When the service was about to start, Mack turned around to see only a small gathering of people.

'Good heavens—they've hardly invited anyone,' he murmured.

'Shh—I think that's how Amanda wanted it,' Jessie whispered.

Pru leaned over and murmured, 'Thank God Tom has shaved off that awful half-beard.'

He appeared clean-shaven in grey flannel trousers and matching waistcoat, and although he was reluctant to wear a black tie, Pru had insisted and he changed his mind.

The nostalgic chapel reminded Mack of the old, white-washed church he attended as a young boy when his mother sent him and Meg to Sunday school. The format of this service appeared to be laid-back, unlike the formal Church of England of his youth.

The organ began bashing out an Air from Bach while Amanda, dressed like a nymph in a simple white dress and gypsophila in her hair walked down the aisle next to her father. Mack looked to make sure she wore shoes and was not barefoot. He elbowed Jessie who forced herself to not laugh out loud.

The ceremony was short and formal. The wedded couple bolted out the door while the organ played on. They couldn't get away quick enough—such a far cry from Jessie and Mack's ceremony which they had planned themselves.

Amanda's folks walked out the door followed by Pru and Wyatt who simultaneously greeted Tom and Amanda with a hug. Tom's new wife seemed to strike up a conversation easily and gravitated towards Jessie. They all stood chatting for a while and then after greeting the guests, the newlyweds made a dash for it.

Tom approached Jessie, 'We're having a barn dance later. Nothing like the elaborate shindig you and Mack had on Reed Station, but we could still have some fun, though. First, a good feed put on by Amanda's folks on the veranda under cover.'

Amanda's mother seemed to be in her element organising everyone. She approached Pru and Wyatt.

'Ah, there you are—good thing we all met at your house last night otherwise this could have been awkward. Are we all ready to go onto the reception yet?'

'Yes, I think we're all sorted, aren't we dear?' Pru looped her arm in Wyatt's as they walked to their vehicles.

It was an afternoon wedding and still warm. They set the food out on a long trestle table covered with a white cloth. With the help of a few friends, multiple dishes of fancy food paid for by Amanda's parents appeared on the tables.

The music from the barn bellowed until midnight and the twins slept through it all while the Mack and Jessie took turns checking on them in the house all evening.

Coloured lights flashed illuminating a dance floor covered in fine sawdust.

'I should have brought my gumboots,' said Wyatt, grinning at his wife.

'Come, dear, let's have one more dance before I head off to bed.' Pru pulled Wyatt back into the middle of the dance floor. Afterwards, they retired to bed early, leaving the young ones to party on.

Later that night, Jessie looked around for Tom and Amanda, but they had disappeared, telling no one. Pru and Wyatt had booked them into an apartment on the ocean side at Mount Maunganui with a sea view for their wedding present. While the newlyweds were away on their honeymoon, Mack and Wyatt monitored the farm, although Tom's farm manager had it under control.

Four days later, the Glenorchy bridal party began their long trip back home. It had been a whirlwind event and Mack didn't enjoy travelling so far from home, for, in the back of his mind, he had reservations about leaving his grandfather.

Chapter Twenty-Six

Jessie yanked off her court shoes and plonked herself down into an armchair, massaging the back of her neck.

'Whew! Thank the Lord the boys went off to sleep straight away—I'm glad we're home.'

Mack carried their suitcases down to the bedroom and returned in his pyjamas.

'What a long trip that was. At least Tom didn't have too far to travel to collect us from Rotorua Airport. It's so good that Mt Cook Airlines are stopping there now and we don't have to commute from Auckland.'

'Yes, it's great—and the twins were much better than I expected. They had everyone in the aircraft fussing over them.'

Mack yawned. 'Tom didn't give people much warning, as our invitations only arrived a month before the wedding. Especially for people like us who had so far to travel.'

Jessie bent down to pick up some of the children's toys off the floor and placed them in their toy basket.

'True—don't you think Amanda is a sweetie? When I first met her, I didn't think she was cut out to be a farmer's wife, but she proved me wrong. Tom said she helped him with lambing and doesn't mind getting her hands dirty. She has her own horse and has won a few prizes at shows.'

Mack sat munching on an apple. 'I'm pleased it was a simple affair. There was only a handful of people—family and close friends which is what they wanted. I thought Amanda was dressed like a nymph,—quite liberal. As long as she is a good match for Tom, that's all that matters—listen—is that one of the boys calling out?'

Jessie tiptoed along the hallway and peeped through the door.

'No, they are sound asleep,' she said walking back and sitting next to Mack again. 'I think it's one of the lambs that Grandad weaned while we were away.'

'Let's get to bed—it won't hurt to have an early night for a change. I've got an early start tomorrow with the shearing contractors arriving first thing,' Mack said, rubbing his eyes.

They turned out the lights and shuffled off down to their bedroom. Jessie sat on the edge of the bed brushing her hair. 'We have to think about what we will do for the twins' first birthday. It will be a busy Christmas this year. Oh ... I'm worn out thinking about it. Time to get some sleep.'

****

Reed station became a flurry of activity during the shearing season. The truck arrived with shearers, shedhands and cooks all bustling about looking for their accommodation—laughing and joking in high spirits.

Jessie bounced Oliver up and down on her knee in a chair by the outdoor table watching the workers come and go while baby Will sat playing in his mobile walker.

Holding a mug of tea, Walter wandered out onto the veranda to observe the activity. Instantly he held a hand against his forehead and started to sway.

'Are you okay, Grandad? Come and sit down.'

Walter slumped back in a wicker chair, leaning forward with his head resting on his hands.

'What's wrong—are you unwell?' Jessie stared at him, her brow crinkling.

'Don't worry about me, lassie. It's just one of those jolly headaches I get now and then,' he mumbled, barely lifting his head.

'Let me get you your painkillers. Where do you keep them?'

'In the medicine cabinet in the bathroom above the hand basin.'

Jessie secured the gate on the veranda to stop Will escaping, propped Oliver on her hip and went looking for the tablets.

She arrived back with a glass of water. Placing Oliver on the ground she pulled the medication from her pocket and handed it to Walter.

'Here, Grandad—you'd better take these. If it doesn't subside, I'll take you in to see the doctor.'

'No need for that now. I'm supposed to be helping Mack and Ben get those sheep into the woolshed race. I said I would be there.'

'You're not going anywhere, Grandad. We don't want you having another stroke. You're supposed to rest when you get these headaches. Have you been taking your blood pressure pills?'

'Yes—and I know all that. But you can't keep a shepherd down—you should know that by now.'

****

Jessie heard the thumping of boots on the veranda steps. It was a warm summer's evening as Mack stumbled in, lifting his arms and sniffing his armpits.

'Bah, that smells high—I'm going straight to the shower.' He began stripping off his black, woollen singlet.

A short time later he came out of the bathroom reeking of aftershave. Jessie walked over and stroked his smooth cheeks.

'Ooh—clean-shaven too. What's the occasion?'

'Nothing—just that it's so dirty in the woolsheds and I feel as though the stench permeates everything.'

Mack always helped Jessie bath the boys. He never once thought it was her role as she was working three jobs.

'I've already run their bath. I'll take Olly.'

Jessie glared at him. 'Please don't start calling him that. It'll stick and Oliver's such a charming name.'

'Okay, you're right. Let's get them into the bath.'

Jessie picked up Will and carried him into the bathroom.

After they bathed the children and tucked them into their cots, Jessie expressed her concerns to Mack about Walter.

'I'm worried about him. You should try and get him to see the doctor—he had a bad headache today and needed pain relief. I thought he was going to pass out.'

'He seemed to be a bit on the slow side with mustering earlier, even though I only gave him a handful to do. Maybe I can take him in to see the doctor late this afternoon. I'll be tied up until then.'

****

The trip to the doctor was a false alarm. All Joshua told him was to rest as he explained that dehydration causes headaches, and he had to drink more water.

In the Ute on the way home, Walter started talking about all the things he'd like to teach the boys.

'I'd like to get two miniature horses, the same as Meg has and then I can teach them how to ride.'

'It's too soon for that yet, Grandad. Perhaps in another couple of years. I'm all for it but not yet. Wait until they're a little older.'

'Well, I don't want to wait too long—I might not be around for too much longer. This old body is decaying.'

Mack's brows snapped together. Don't be ridiculous—we're all decaying. Isn't that what the pastor said in the sermon on Sunday? Anyway—the doctor thinks you're as fit as a flea.'

'I'm not sure about that. I know what my body is telling me.'

After dropping his father back home, Mack climbed on his quad bike and rode off to check the calves.

Jessie agreed to let the boys sit with Walter on the tractor parked near the house where she could see them. They loved him a great deal, especially when he spent so much time with them.

Chapter Twenty-Seven

Two years later - 1986

Mack had the day off. After a belly full of Christmas cake and apple cider, he rested on the couch in the living room, reading a book by one of his favourite Suspense authors.

Jessie yawned as she reached to pick up one of Will's Tonka trucks off the floor. 'We must teach our boys to put their own toys away. I'm worn out and never thought I'd be pleased to have the house to ourselves, but today I'm glad of it.'

'They were spoilt rotten by their grandparents this Christmas. Look at how many toys they gave them. I hope they get to play with them all, but I doubt it. I think they would rather be outside with the animals with me or Grandad on the farm.'

'Where are they right now? I can't see them in the yard.' Jessie hurried over to the window.

Mack yawned and put down his book. 'Grandad took them out to show them how to feed the lambs from that dead ewe. He made a temporary pen for them in the front yard. Do you mind if I take a short nap? I need to recharge my batteries.'

'No, you have a rest. I'll just be fussing around here keeping tabs on the boys, and that includes our big boy out there.' Jessie chuckled.

She went out through the front door to look for them and heard the lambs crying for their mother. The boys stood watching their great-grandfather coax the animals to take the teat from the bottle of warm milk.

Jessie, satisfied that they were in good hands, went back inside to tidy up.

Bessie was away with her family for the holidays which meant Mack and Jessie had all the housework and cooking to do between them. Walter just wasn't up to much anymore. He showed signs of slowing down.

Jessie dusted and vacuumed Walter's room. She was about to wipe down his bedside table when she discovered a book of memoirs like the ones she'd seen about the Reed family in Arrowtown Historical Museum lying on his dresser. She opened the book to see a chronological history of the gold miners, Mack's ancestors. There was a photo of the original homestead before they rebuilt it and an aerial view of the station. Jessie found the black and white photos of Walter's parents and grandparents in authentic vintage clothing intriguing. A large coloured photo on the bedside table caught her eye. It was a handsome woman with long, jet black hair pulled softly back into a simple braid, and a long, blue dress. Hazel Reed stood in the forefront of the original Reed Station homestead.

She heard a voice and promptly closed the book, dragging the vacuum cleaner into the hallway to see Will standing there.

'Mummy! Poppa showed us how to feed Barney and Lofty. He said we can do it all by ourselves now. Come and watch us.'

Before Jessie could reply, Will bounded back out the door while his mother stood at the window smiling warmly at the boys showing their skills with a milk bottle. She waved and gave a thumbs-up of approval.

Walter, convinced that he'd taught them sufficiently how to get the lambs to take the teat and the right way to hold the milk bottle, went back up on the veranda to watch them from under the outdoor umbrella. He wiped his brow with his handkerchief and closed his eyes. Jessie stood in the living room window briefly, smiling at the sight of her three-year-old twin boys feeding twin lambs while their Poppa looked on. After she finished the vacuuming, Jessie set up the iron board and before she turned the iron on, a commotion startled her. Her sons shouted out at and as she looked up, the two of them barged through the door, trying to catch their breath.

'Mummy! We want Poppa to help us but he won't open his eyes,' cried Oliver. 'Can you tell him to wake up?'

'Yes, Mummy, quick—come! Lofty wants more milk and Poppa said he would get more if it runs out,' said Will, pulling her other arm.

Jessie almost toppled the ironing board. She switched off the iron and followed them onto the veranda.

'Quiet—don't wake him if he's taking a nap. It looks like he's exhausted. It's good you came to tell me though. You can't stay out here on your own.'

Jessie peered at Walter as she reached up to change the slant of the umbrella to screen his face from the sun. Suddenly she braced herself and took a step back, squinting from the glare. Edging her way along the table where he sat, she froze.

Her face paled as she bent down to speak to her sons.

'Please go inside and wake Daddy ... tell him I need him right now—go!'

The twins stood gaping then ran inside the house.

Jessie turned to Walter. 'Grandad, wake up! Please, Grandad, open your eyes!' she yelled.

Walter lay motionless, about to slide off the seat. Jessie pressed her knuckles hard into his breastbone while he remained deathly still. She leaned over, touching his mouth with her left cheek. 'Oh, no. Please, not now!' Her eyes welled up as she held his cold hand. He had already gone.

Mack rushed out onto the veranda.

'I'm so sorry, darling but Grandad's ... he's gone. Tell the boys to stay in the living room then help me.'

After helping Jessie slide him off his chair and onto the floor, Mack raced back to her side after he rang the flying doctor.

'Shall we start CPR?'

'I'm sorry, darling, it's too late. He died peacefully in his sleep watching his grandsons feeding their lambs.'

Mack burst into tears. Not so much because of Walter's death, as he knew the eighty-six-year-old had lived on borrowed time following two strokes, but more so because he never had the chance to say goodbye.

Jessie took Mack's hand. 'You know our boys have had a privileged relationship with Grandad and so have we. He enhanced our lives so much and I hope he knew how much we appreciated him.'

They both kissed him on the forehead and covered him with a blanket. Jessie wrapped her arms around Mack then called the boys who came running back with exuberance. Mack guessed they expected to see their Poppa sitting up talking.

Will tugged on Jessie's sleeve. 'Why is Poppa lying on the ground—why doesn't he wake up, Mummy? He said we could give Lofty and Barney another bottle. Please wake him for us.'

Jessie gathered the children together under her arms. They snuggled into her.

'Poppa is in a deep sleep and won't wake anymore until he is with God in Heaven. He's waiting for him and the helicopter will take him there.'

'But why is he going away—we don't want him to go?' said Oliver, teary-eyed.

'Sometimes God just lends us people so we can love them and they can love us back. Then he gives them to others for a while. It's someone else's turn to love Poppa now. One day we'll all be together again when he has finished working for God.'

'He's freezing, Mummy,' wailed Oliver. 'Can the blanket make him better?'

'When the helicopter gets here they will take him to a place where he will never be cold again.'

'The helicopter will take him to God, won't it?' Will asked, staring at the shape under the blanket.

'Yes, my darling. He's going to heaven where all good shepherds live. There'll be lots of lambs for him to take care of there.'

Both boys walked up to the lifeless form covered by the blanket and lay across him with their heads on his chest.

'Don't worry, Poppa. We know how to give Barney and Lofty their milk so they won't be hungry while you're away. You wait for us, promise?' The roar of the helicopter's rotors drowned out Oliver's voice as it landed in the field next to the homestead.

As the air ambulance officers took Walter on a stretcher out to the helicopter with its engine still roaring, Mack stood on the veranda fighting back more tears. He and Jessie held the hands of their children saying a silent goodbye.

'Daddy—Mummy said you're a good shepherd. Are you going to go off with Poppa too?' Will gazed at him with wide eyes.

'No, I'm not going anywhere until I'm old like Poppa and you'll be grown up. We'll all see Poppa in God's pastures and he'll be teaching other children to feed the lambs and find those that have strayed and lost their way.'

They all stood huddled together on the veranda as the helicopter churned its way into the sky with Oliver and Will blowing butterfly kisses until it disappeared behind the clouds.

****

EPILOGUE

Walter's funeral service was held at the Glenorchy chapel. Following his request, after his cremation, the family took his ashes, as he had requested to be buried in a plot at the Church of the Good Shepherd at Lake Tekapo next to his wife, Hazel. His family travelled to see the gravestone they had got engraved.

WALTER JOHN REED
THE GOOD SHEPHERD 1900 -1986
HUSBAND OF HAZEL, FATHER OF LEN,
GRANDFATHER OF MACK AND MEG AND GREAT-
GRANDFATHER OF WILL AND OLIVER. HE PASSED
AWAY DOING WHAT HE LOVED MOST. MAY YOU REST
IN PEACE. YOU WILL BE FOREVER IN OUR HEARTS.

KEEP IN TOUCH

Please visit my website and sign up to my mailing list to hear about new books, sneak previews and giveaways.
www.patriciasnelling.com

Author Bio

Patricia, known as Trish grew up in a small town in New Zealand. From the age of five, she rode horses which her family owned and trained, often winning prizes in the local horse shows. During her early life, her parents lived off the land, initially share-milking and later as horticulturalists.

After completing her nursing studies and qualifying as a Registered Nurse, Patricia spent six years abroad, living in Australia and Europe doing a variety of jobs between her nursing roles and returned to Auckland to start a family. After a forty-year nursing career Patricia retired and now writes inspirational Cosy Mysteries, Adventure and Romantic Suspense set in beautiful New Zealand

www.ingramcontent.com/pod-product-compliance
Lightning Source LLC
Chambersburg PA
CBHW021405290426
44108CB00010B/399